Spice it Up!
An Herbal Extravaganza

A collection of folklore, poems and history of 52
herbs designed to inspire your creative writing

By Iris Craver

Cover Design by Care Connet

ISBN:978109531280^

D1409959

Dedication

My mother, Eileen Craver, tended the herbs at Shaw's Garden for 40 years with the St. Louis Herb Society. She always had a patch of herbs growing outside her kitchen window. Even as she spent her final days in a nursing home, she had small pots of basil and dill and oregano sitting in the window of her room. As a child, I thought that everyone grew up with plantain tinctures for bug bites and chamomile teas to relax and aromatic curry powders for cooking. I dedicate this book to her.

I want to also thank these other herbalists who have shared their love of herbs with me: Ocoee Miller, JoAnn Bauman, Tamara Ishmael-Fairbanks, Audrey Klopper, Sheri Brody, Kimberly Anderson and Rosemary Gladstar.

What's this Book about?

This is not an ordinary book about herbs. This is a book for people who love herbs and also love writing. When I speak about herbalism, I am thinking about people who use plants to improve overall health and wellness. Herbalism is a way of life that brings us closer to the spiritual elements of earth, air, fire and water. We grow our herbs with the help of the earth, the sun and the rain. We breathe the essence of our herbs when we cook or when we make a nice cup of tea or when we make a fragrant posie. Herbalism helps to create a life that is meaningful. Working with herbs is a continuous discovery. Herbalism connects us to our source of life.

Expressive writing is another way of life that brings us closer to discovering the creative spark we each hold. My desire is that this journaling guide will be a useful tool for your herbalism journey and will plant seeds of creativity. What you will find here are some interesting tidbits, stories, poems, and folklore about

52 different herbs; one for each week of the year. And for each herb, you will find seven writing prompts; one for each day of the week. If the writing prompt inspires you, great! If not, write about something else that is on your mind. Let your words take you to interesting places. Spice it up! Treat your words with loving care. I hope you find as much pleasure using this guide as I did in creating it!

I have included information about how these herbs are used for health and wellness. Of course, these are just suggestions based on old knowledge about each of our plant allies. Use them wisely. Err on the side of caution.

Throughout the guide, you will find references to journaling methods I learned from my mentor, Kay Adams. In *The Way of the Journal: A Journal Therapy Workbook for Healing*, she suggested numerous techniques which will facilitate your journaling practice.

THE JOURNALING GLOSSARY

A **Sentence Stem** is a sentence completion process where you fill in the blank with a word or a phrase.

The **Five-Minute Sprint** is for those times when you don't feel like you have time to write.

Clustering is where you put a central word or phrase in the middle of your page and then connect to words that you associate with the main idea. You can then connect all of these words with lines, sort of creating a word map, if you will.

Lists can open up your thoughts on a certain topic without feeling like you need to pay attention to such matters as sentence structure or grammar!

Alpha poems involve writing letters down the side of a page and then writing a poem using the letter for the first word on each line. Alpha poems are a surprising way to begin writing poetry if you think you are not a poet.

Captured Moments create a snapshot of a memory with words.

Writing a **Letter** (which may be sent or unsent) is a familiar form that people find easy to use.

A **Character Sketch** creates a portrait of another person, place or a thing. You can write a "Character Sketch" about Gratitude, for example. What would Gratitude eat for breakfast? What does Gratitude where s/he goes walking? And so on.

A **Dialogue** is an imagined conversation written in two voices. It can be a conversation with your Grandmother or your Greatest Fear.

A **Springboard** is a free write using a quote or a poem or a word or an idea as a prompt.

Anise

The botanical names of anise is Pimpinella anisum. It is said to help with digestion and to sweeten the breath. Anise is used in cough mixtures and lozenges. It is also antiseptic, and a few seeds taken with water will often cure hiccoughs.

~Day 1~

Builders of steam locomotives in Britain incorporated aniseed oil into bearings so the distinctive smell would give warning of overheating according to *Railway Magazine* (1953). Write about train travel or about using distinctive smells as a warning!

~Day 2~

Aniseed has an anethole-like odor and a sweet "licorice-like" taste, which has led to the traditional use of anise oils in licorice candy. Some people love licorice and others, well, not so much. Tom White quotes, "Swimming is like licorice. You either love it or hate it." Write about how you feel about licorice, or swimming!

~Day 3~

Anise is said to increase psychic abilities. Write a short story about someone who uses anise to increase their psychic abilities.

~Day 4~

In a pillow, anise is said to ward off nightmares. See if you can write down your dreams when you wake up in the morning. Set an intention when you go to bed the night before to remember your dreams and then when you first open your eyes in the morning, make sure you have paper and pencil ready to jot down your dream.

~Day 5~

A quote from *The Kitchen Garden*, published in 1861, notes that anise "seeds are much used by distillers to give flavour to cordial liqueurs." Write about your favorite recipe using anise for flavoring. Or, if you have not yet done so, find a recipe, try it out and then write about your experience.

~Day 6~

Anise is an effective bait for rats and mice. What stories do you have to tell about your encounters with rats or mice?

~Day 7~

"Snow must be walked through, felt on the skin, whether tuft or filament, stitch or tear,
a sudden freshness like anise on the tongue." ~ Joyce Wilson. Write your own poem using the word "anise".

Apple

The botanical name for apple is Pyrus malus. Apples eaten at bedtime every night will cure some of the worst forms of constipation. The apple will also act as an excellent dental aid. In addition, apple cider vinegar is thought have healing and cleansing properties, it can be used as a natural antibiotic and can improve digestion and may help with weight loss.

~Day 1~

According to the Smell and Taste Treatment and Research Foundation of Chicago, the smell of green apples helps relieve claustrophobia. Use this sentence stem as a prompt for your writing today - "The smell of apples......."

~Day 2~

John Chapman (1774-1845), more commonly known as Johnny Appleseed has been enshrined in American historical, literary, and folk tradition. He won the respect of settlers and Native Americans alike as he made his way from his native Massachusetts to the Pennsylvania/ Ohio/Indiana frontier, planting apple trees. He exchanged his apple seeds and seedlings for what he needed to live. Visit an apple orchard or tree near where you live. Write about your experience spending time with an apple tree.

~Day 3~

Two pounds of apples make one 9-inch pie. Write a story about a favorite memory you have of eating apple pie.

~Day 4~

The old saying, "An apple a day, keeps the doctor away." Make up a new idiom using the sentence stem, "An apple a day........."

~Day 5~

Another popular saying is "You are the apple of my eye". Write a character sketch of someone who is the apple of your eye.

~Day 6~

"If I knew the world would end tomorrow, I would still plant apple trees today" ~ Martin Luther. Such a message of hope! Write about what you do in your life to sustain a sense of hope.

~Day 7~

The apple has long been considered in folklore to a symbol for love. Write to someone you love and be certain to use the word "apple" somewhere in the letter.

Basil

The botanical name for basil is Ocymum basilium. Basil is an important medicinal plant in various traditional and folk systems of medicines, such as those in Southeast Asia and India. Basil can help to reduce inflammation, pain, fever and stress. It is considered to protect the liver, blood vessels and boost the immune system.

~Day 1~

"A man taking basil from a woman will love her always." quoted Sir Thomas Moore. Make a list of the ones you would give some basil so that they would love you always. This can be friends, family members, neighbors or even pets!

~Day 2~

European folklore includes carrying a sprig of basil in your pocket to bring wealth, sprinkling it on the floor to ward off evil and setting it near doors and cash registers to attract customers. If basil helps you attract wealth and ward off evil, write about what happens the day you wake up and discover this is true!

~Day 3~

Napoleon used basil for its property of stimulating intellectual concentration. What is of interest to you that calls for more stimulating intellectual concentration? For example, I would like to learn to speak Spanish and would like to concentrate on this study more regularly. Write about your topic of interest.

~Day 4~

Small pots of basil were given as parting gifts to guests to bless their journeys. Think about the last guest who visited your home. Write a character sketch of that person.

~Day 5~

"Where salt is good, so is basil." ~ Italian saying. Write a conversation between salt and basil.

~Day 6~

Basil has a lovely fragrance. Put in water for a few days as you would cut flowers! Use this sentence stem as your writing prompt today - "The fragrance of basil………."

~Day 7~

After arguing with a loved one, take time to calm down while sipping basil tea. Serve meals heavily laced with basil during times of family strife to help with reconciliation. Write about keeping the peace over a cup of basil tea.

Bay Leaf

The botanical name for bay leaf is Laurus nobilis. Bay leaves have been used for healing wounds, helping with digestion, relieving dandruff, and reducing bloating. It is said that placing a bay leaf in front of your nose will help get rid of headaches. The essential oil can be used to massage muscle aches and pains and ease arthritis.

~Day 1~

Wreaths made of bay leaves were used by the Greeks to decorate the heads of heroic citizens. If you were going to place a bay leaf wreath on someone to honor them, who would it be? Write about this person and why you would want to honor them.

~Day 2~

Tossing bay leaves into a fire will make firecracker sounds. Write an alpha poem using the word "firecracker". See if you can make the poem sound like firecrackers. See if you can somehow include a reference to bay leaves in your poem.

~Day 3~

Bay leaf burning has long been used as a way to relieve stress. Chemicals in the leaves creates a smoke that, when inhaled, can be calming. Write down some of the stresses you have in your life. After burning a bay leaf, also burn your paper and let the ashes carry your stresses away on the breeze.

~Day 4~

The world laureate as in poet laureate and baccalaureate and the term "to rest on one's laurels" are additional reminders of the high status of this tree. Find out who is the poet laureate for your state or country. Write them a letter expressing appreciation for their contributions.

~Day 5~

It is said that if you write a wish on a dried bay leaf and then burn it and your wish will come true. Do this!

~Day 6~

Early Greeks and Romans associated the bay laurel with Apollo, the patron god of music and poetry. Make a gratitude list for music and poetry. Think of as many ways that music and poetry play a part in your life.

~Day 7~

Bay leaves are found in symbols around the world, such as the American dollar bill, the 10 yen coin of Japan, the shield and flag of the Dominican Republic and it is even the clan plant of the Scottish clan Graham. It is very important in Greece where it is found as the national emblem of the country. Create a symbol for yourself using a bay leaf. How will you use this symbol in your life?

Black pepper

The botanical name for black pepper is Piper nigrum. Because of its stimulant action, black pepper can help digestion and an upset stomach. It has also been used for vertigo and arthritis. Black pepper helps with circulation and can possibly help with lowering high blood pressure.

~Day 1~

The Romans loved adding pepper to their food; in fact, in the oldest known cookbook in existence, 80 percent of the recipes contain the spice. Look in one of your cookbooks and find a recipe calling for the use of black pepper. Make the dish, eat it and write about it!

~Day 2~

Black pepper is spicy, feels earthy and grounding. It is thought to strengthen your ability to express yourself. Try sprinkling some pepper on a page of your journal and then write a list of words that come to your mind when you think about expressing the things or ideas that matter to you.

~Day 3~

During the 5th century CE, Attila the Hun demanded 3,000 pounds of pepper as a ransom for the city of Rome. What would you trade for a pound of pepper? Write a short story or a poem or a song about a pound of pepper.

~Day 4~

Black pepper is called the "King of Spices" and is the world's most commonly traded spice. If black pepper is the king of spices, what would be the "Queen of Spices". What herb or spice would you consider to the queen? Scribe a proclamation declaring this herb or spice the Queen and proclaim how she relates to black pepper, the King!

~Day 5~

"Peppering your relationship with a dash of mystery can make it far more palatable." ~ Khang Kijarro Nguyen. Use this as a springboard for your writing today - "Peppering your........."

~Day 6~

Through the early 20th century, the word pepper was shortened to the slang word "pep" to describe a person full of spirit and energy. Make a list of 31 things, people or places or activities that give you "pep", spirit, and energy. Then, if today is the 7th and you listed "swimming" as number 7 on your list, write about how swimming gives you "pep".

~Day 7~

Burning black pepper before smudging your home with sage is a powerful combination. The black pepper will help remove negative energies. Smudging is an ancient practice in many cultures and spiritual traditions. If you don't want to burn pepper or sage to smudge your home, you could just sprinkle some in the corners or around the perimeter of the house. Here is a smudging prayer ~ Smoke of air and fire of earth, cleanse and bless this home and hearth. Drive away all harm and fear, only good may enter here. Now, write your own smudging prayer.

Borage

The botanical name for borage is Borago officinalis. Borage can be helpful in dealing with inflammation, skin disorders, fatigue, stress, arthritis pain, colds, coughs, fever and bronchitis.

~Day 1~

Being around borage is said to strengthen the heart. Borage is good for passions of the heart. What is your heart's passion? Write about it.

~Day 2~

The name borage could originate from the Celtic *barrach*, a man of courage. Here is a poem I wrote titled *Courage:*

"Courage wears red underpants.
She never gets heartburn even when she eats greasy tacos.
Every day, she gets up, makes her bed, does the dishes, goes to work and pays her bills.
When someone in her family is having a hard time, she makes sure to call and check in,
even if it's uncomfortable to talk about whatever's going on.
Courage and Love are best friends.
Most of the time, others think they're not for real.
It doesn't matter.
Courage can move quickly when she needs to.
She can also sit for a very long time next to the bed of someone who is dying.
Every so often,
if she's not exactly sure what to do,
she calls Love on the phone
and gets reminded......"do what you know is right in your heart".

Write your own poem about courage.

~Day 3~

The pretty blue flowers have been added to salads since Elizabethan times to "make the mind glad." Write a verse using the word glad, pretty, salad, flowers, blue and mind.

~Day 4~

Frozen inside of ice cubes, borage flowers make an unusual garnish for summer drinks. Write a short story about spending a summer day with your favorite drink cooled by borage flower ice cubes.

~Day 5~

Use borage in your bath to help you in a difficult situation. If you are having some difficulty, do you like to soak in the tub or do you prefer to wash away your troubles with a shower? Write about the joys of a good soak or the pleasures of a nice shower.

~Day 6~

Susan Kinsolving wrote a bit of prose titled *"Parliament Passes The Inclosing Lands Act, 1809"* in which she describes the loss for a man who loved to wander and hike about on the ancient old footpaths. An excerpt reads:

"The open-field system would end. Every acre was enumerated in a way John Clare could not comprehend. Why should footpaths have fences, streams be made straight, why fell trees, wall a field and lock it with a gate? No longer could he drink from Eastwell spring; the bubbling water was penned by scaffolding. *No Trespassing* at every turn, posted over scurvy-grass, loosestrife, vetch, clover, and fern. Clare doffed his cap and wept for his right to roam; in chicory, thistle, briony and buttercup, he'd always been at home. Or coming upon a gypsy camp (fires and tambourines!) he'd share his fleabane, borage, parsley, some beans."

Write about what you like to share around the campfire.

~Day 7~

It is recommended to meditate with the borage plant when are feeling heavyhearted. The longer you meditate upon the borage plant, the more you can feel lightness and upliftment soothing your heart. Find a picture of borage and gaze at the image as a meditation. Write about your meditation and any messages you received from borage.

Calendula

The botanical name for calendula is Calendula officianalis. It is also known as English marigold, however, it is not the same as the Mexican marigold with the botanical name of Tagetes erecta. The calendula petals have been found to promote wound-healing and may aid in the treatment of acute dermatitis. The flowers may be useful in reducing abdominal cramps and constipation. Calendula extract can also be effective as an insecticide.

~Day 1~

Calendula is the traditional "he loves me, he loves me not" flower and is useful for love potions. Write up your own recipe for a love potion.

~Day 2~

Calendula is associated with the Sun. What do you like to do on a sunny day? Write about it.

~Day 3~

In some cultures, calendula is a symbol of endurance, alluding to its ability to bloom for so long. Write a poem about endurance. See if you fit the word "calendula" into your poem.

~Day 4~

In German folklore, rain was predicted if the calendula flowers remained closed after 9 a.m. What do you like to do on a rainy day? Write about it.

~Day 5~

Here is a recipe for a facial scrub using 1 cup of oatmeal, ½ cup of cornmeal and 1/3 cup of dried calendula. Grind the ingredients in an electric coffee grinder to a fine powder. Store in a closed container. To use the scrub, make a paste of 1 teaspoon scrub powder and enough water to moisten and apply to a dampened face. Gently scrub face and rinse with warm water. Try it out and then write about what you see in the mirror after you do this scrub!

~Day 6~

Calendula exhibits a strange sensitivity to light from the sun. Old time farmers and gardeners knew that the flower opened its half-shut eyes each day about 9 a.m. For about six hours it slowly turned its head to follow the bright sun. Around 3 p.m., it began folding its petals for another night of slumber.   What time do you open your eyes in the morning? And what time do you fold up for another night of slumber? Write about what you did yesterday in between opening your eyes and folding for the night.

~Day 7~

Sometimes described as "the flower of grief," droplets gather in the flower during the night and drip off like tears when it opens in the morning. This characteristic moved Shakespeare to write in *A Winter's Tale*: "The Marigold that goes to bed with the sun, / And with him rises weeping." Have you ever woken up crying? Write about something that makes you that sad. A bit of caution here! Don't spend more than 15 minutes writing about such grief. James Pennebaker, a pre-eminent researcher on the use of therapeutic writing, advises not to spend extensive time writing about grief as it reinforces neural pathways in the brain that may not be beneficial. However, a short time spent writing about such losses can be helpful.

Caraway

The botanical name for caraway is Carum carvi. Caraway stimulates digestion and also can promote milk production for nursing mothers. It can help to soothe colic in babies. A poultice made from the seeds can relieve bruises.

~Day 1~

An old legend is that any object containing a few caraway seeds would be kept safe from theft. What special item do you own? Can you tape some caraway seeds to the bottom of your treasure to keep it safe? Write about why this object is important to you!

~Day 2~

In Scotland, a small plate of caraway seed is put down at tea to dip the buttered side of bread into and called 'salt water jelly.' Try out a buttered slice of bread with some salt water jelly. Write about eating bread and butter. With jelly?

~Day 3~

Caraway is used to prevent fowls and pigeons from straying. Pigeons, who are particularly fond of the seeds, will never stray if they are given a piece of baked caraway dough. Write an alpha poem using the word *"pigeon"*. See if you can work the word "caraway" into your pigeon poem.

~Day 4~

The comedian, Fred Allen, commented that "All the sincerity in Hollywood you could stuff in a flea's navel and still have room left to conceal eight caraway seeds and an agent's heart." Do a 5-minute writing sprint using the word - "Sincerity........."

~Day 5~

The seed of the caraway plant is excellent to use for protection against negativity. Make a list of people, places and things that create negativity in your life. Close your eyes and put your finger on the list. Then, write about what your life might be like without this negative energy.

~Day 6~

"A little beer would suit me better, if it's all the same to you, my good sir," said Balin with the white beard. "But I don't mind some cake - seed-cake if you have any." "Lots!" Bilbo found himself answering, to his own surprise; and he found himself scuttling off, too, to the cellar to fill a pint beer-mug, and to the pantry to fetch two beautiful round seed-cakes which he had baked that afternoon for his after-supper morsel."~ From *The Hobbit,* by J.R.R. Tolkien, Chapter One. Write about spending an afternoon eating caraway seed cakes with hobbits!

~Day 7~

Wearing a cloth bag filled with caraway seeds is thought to improve memory. Pick a memory from the last week or month or year and write about it.

Cayenne

The botanical name for cayenne is Capsicum minimum. A natural painkiller found in cayenne, helps treat muscle soreness and skin infections. It helps reduce weight by increasing your metabolism. It can help to eliminate artery wall plaque.

~Day 1~

"If you master only *one* herb in your life, master cayenne pepper. It is *more* powerful than any other." ~ Dr. Schulze, a well-known herbal healer. Cayenne is clearly Dr. Schulze's favorite herb. Most people have a favorite. Write about your favorite herb.

~Day 2~

"I actually start my day with a cup of warm lemon water with cayenne pepper. It jump-starts your detoxifying system in your body, jump-starts your liver, helps you eliminate the food that you ate the day before, and also just gets your body in an alkaline state ready to ward off disease." ~ Vani Hari. Write about the first hour of a typical day for you.

~Day 3~

Cayenne is considered to symbolize fidelity. Fidelity means loyalty or faithfulness. Write a short story about being loyal using a character by the name of Cayenne.

~Day 4~

An epulaerya is a poem about food. The poem structure consists of lines with syllables as follows: 7/5/7/5/5/3/1. Write an epulaerya about cayenne.

~Day 5~

"How do I love thee? Let me count the ways. I love thee more than cayenne pepper, which sets my heart ablaze." ~ A Louisiana love poem. Write about love that is as hot as cayenne!

~Day 6~

An excerpt from a poem written by Rhonda Johnson-Saunders, titled *Life Is Like A Maypole*, reads:

"Spring bows to thrill of cayenne summer,

dreams spiced in youthful glow come May.

Bright ribbons wake my bare feet's slumber.

Spring bows to thrill of cayenne summer!

Rainbow pleats dance, no clouds encumber

my twirling limbs, life's weaved sashay.

Spring bows to thrill of cayenne summer,

dreams spiced in youthful glow come May!"

Close your eyes and point your finger at these words. If your finger lands on the word *"rainbow"*, write about *rainbows*!

~Day 7~

Meri Culp wrote a poem titled *Cayenne Warning*. Here are a few lines:

"Even the pepper's skin will burn to the touch, Mom,
my son says as he fingers the slim fire, the just-picked
red ripeness. Be careful, he reminds, all kindness,
newfound protection, as I watch him harvest the
peppers, red-handed, soon-to-be a man.
I want to tell him of life's red hot sting,
of his grandmother's dying request
for me to paint her fingernails chili pepper red."

Write about "life's red hot sting".

Chamomile

The botanical name for chamomile is Anthemis nobilis. In traditional folk medicine, it has been widely used as a sedative and tonic. Chamomile has also been used to treat depression, stress, teething and colic. It is believed to calm the digestive system.

~Day 1~

Scatter chamomile around your property for use in protection against lightning strikes. Think back on a time when you saw lightning strike and heard the thunder that followed. Tell the story of this storm.

~Day 2~

In an excerpt from the poem titled *"Chamomile Tea"* by Katherine Mansfield, she says:

"How little I thought, a year ago,
That he and I should be sitting so
And sipping a cup of chamomile tea.

We might be fifty, we might be five,
So snug, so compact, so wise are we!
Under the kitchen-table leg
My knee is pressing against his knee. "

What is happening in your life now that you did not anticipate a year ago? Write about it.

~Day 3~

Folklore advises to place chamomile flowers in your wallet to attract money. Suppose you do? What would you do with the money chamomile attracted for you? Write about it.

~Day 4~

Chamomile has used by gardeners through the ages and has been called the plant's physician. Nothing contributes so much to the health of a garden as chamomile planted all around. If another plant is drooping and sickly, in nine cases out of ten, it will recover if you place a chamomile plant near it. When you are drooping or sickly, what helps you feel better? Make a list of 31 things that you can do to help you recover when you are not well. Then, let's say that today is the 13th day of the month and you listed *"Watch movies"* as number 13 on your list. Write about how *watching movies* helps you feel better.

~Day 5~

When walked on, chamomiles strong, fragrant apple scent will often reveal its presence before it is seen. Walking over the plant seems especially beneficial to it. Walking on chamomile seems to help it grow and spread. Walking is good for us too! Write a letter of gratitude to Walking.

~Day 6~

Here is a bit of another poem titled *Chamomile* by Marisa Lishay:

"Soft like chamomile, sweet like rain,

giving my heart to you has never been in vain."

Try filling in these blanks -

"_____ like chamomile

_____ like rain

Giving my heart _____."

~Day 7~

"The best rainy evening dilemma: chamomile or earl grey." ~Terri Guillemets. OK, it's another stormy rainy writing prompt! On a rainy evening, let's say you choose chamomile tea over earl grey. Then what happens? Write about it.

Chickweed

The botanical name for chickweed is Stellaria media. People take chickweed for constipation, stomach and bowel problems, blood disorders, asthma, diseases, obesity, psoriasis, rabies, itching, and joint pain.

~Day 1~

Although chickweed is native to Europe, its seeds have traveled far and wide to every corner of the planet. If you could travel far and wide like chickweed, where would you like to go? Write about what attracts you to this place.

~Day 2~

Chickweed seeds can remain fertile and germinate for up to 40 years, and even through a tough winter, she can still survive and thrive. Chickweed is persistence. Write a letter to yourself with advice from chickweed on how to endure and sustain energy to thrive.

~Day 3~

It is said that spending time around chickweed gives us the inner strength. Make a word map placing "Inner strength" in the middle of your page. Jot down words that come to mind as you think of inner strength. See where these words take you.

~Day 4~

Chickweed prefers to grow in groups and clusters, but even within these clusters each flower maintains its own individuality, and shares space neatly with every other cluster of flowers on the plant. Chickweed teaches us to live in balance with ourselves and those around us. Think about a time that you have shared space with others. Write about what lessons you have learned about living in balance with yourself and people in your community.

~Day 5~

In the first lines of a poem titled "*Chickweed*" by Lisa Esposito Faraone, she joyfully expresses:

"In the spring I see you,
winking at me.
Reminding me of my connection
to earth, to myself."

Write your own poem about chickweed using Faraone's first line - "In the spring I see you..."

~Day 6~

"She dreamed that night of chickweed, which was a strange thing to dream about. Chickweed is a low, weedy little plant, not very distinguished. No one writes poetry comparing their lovers to chickweed (or if they do, the poems are rarely well received)." ~ T. Kingfisher. Write another poem comparing someone you love to chickweed.

~Day 7~

The botanical name Stellaria comes from the Latin for *star* and refers to the tiny white, star-shaped flowers. Remember the nursery rhyme?

"Star bright, star light. First star I've seen tonight. Wish I may, wish I might. Have the wish I wish tonight."

Make a wish upon a star tonight and write about what your life would be like if this wish comes true!

Cinnamon

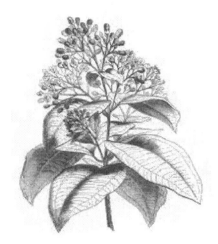

The botanical name for cinnamon is Cinnamomum zeylanicum. Cinnamon almost has super powers! It may reduce inflammation and lowers cholesterol and blood pressure. Cinnamon is thought to increase circulation and aid in tissue repair. It is said to improve the health of the colon and the brain.

~Day 1~

You can use cinnamon to erase scrapes, scuffs, and scratches on wooden furniture. Think of your favorite piece of wooden furniture. Write a character sketch of this piece of furniture. What would it tell you if it could talk?

~Day 2~

Put cinnamon sticks as air freshener in your car. It will smell lovely and as a bonus, the scent of cinnamon has been shown to improve alertness and reduce anxiety making the drive less stressful! Where did you go the last time you drove or took a ride in a car? Write about it. Could be a road trip or even just a trip to the grocery.

~Day 3~

You can also place a cinnamon stick around the kitchen to discourage ants. Make a list of 10 questions you have about ants. Do some research and then write about what you learned.

~Day 4~

"The heady scent of cinnamon, upon the opening of the door, the tugging out of memories, from the mind's musty store" ~ David Whalen. Write about one of your own cinnamon memories.

~Day 5~

"I really don't think I need buns of steel. I'd be happy with buns of cinnamon." ~ Ellen DeGeneres. Use this as a spring board for your writing today.

~Day 6~

Here is a recipe for making cinnamon clay:

Ingredients:

1 cup Applesauce
1/3 cup White Glue
Any combination of ground Cloves, ground Nutmeg, ground allspice, and/or ground ginger to equal 1 cup
1/2 cup of ground cinnamon
More Cinnamon

In a medium bowl, stir together all of the spices. Mix in the applesauce and glue. Work the mixture with hands for 2-3 minutes to form a firm ball. If it's too wet, add more cinnamon, if it's too dry, add more applesauce. Lightly dust a surface with cinnamon. Roll the dough ¼ inch thick if cutting shapes. Or mold with hands. Small shapes are best. Dry in the oven at 200 degrees for several hours or air dry in a sunny spot for a week.

Whatever you decide to make with your clay, embellish it with some of your favorite words. You can carve them into the clay with a toothpick!

~Day 7~

In Southern Illinois, where my kinfolk have lived for generations, people dab a little cinnamon on a wart and say that it will disappear overnight! A Japanese folk story tells about an old man who had a wart on the side of his face. It was the size of a peach. It hurt, but he never complained. One day he was up in the mountains, cutting wood, when a dreadful storm arose. He had never been in such a storm before. The old man heard voices of the Storm Spirits. They sat in a circle around a fire and sang. The old man could not sit still. He sprang into the midst of the group and began to dance. Then the Storm Spirits said: "Oh, good man, you have made us so happy dancing for us. In return, we will take away that terrible wart on the side of your face and so they did. When he reached home his wife cried, "Oh, husband, what have you done with your wart?" Then he told her all about it, and they were very glad and lived happily ever after.

Now, write your own folk story about cinnamon or about warts!

Cleavers

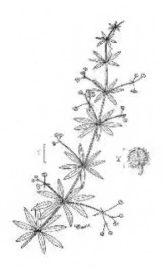

The botanical name for cleavers is Galium aparine. Cleavers can help relieve insomnia and create a quiet, restful sleep. As a poultice, cleavers are useful for healing sores and blisters. The early shoots, rich in vitamin C, are used as a spring tonic.

~Day 1~

"My first encounter with cleavers happened at a very young age. I remember it well. I went with my great Aunt Bett up in the mountains in search of them. I didn't really know what I was looking for, I was just following along with Aunt Bett when I fell flat on my face. She picked me up and with her pristine handkerchief that lived in her apron pocket, she wiped away the tears and the dirt. "I knew if I brought you with me, you would help me find them cleavers, chile, you done good!" A cleavers magnet, that's what I am, and always have been." ~ Sharon Brown. Is there anything in your life that you attract as though you were a magnet? Write about what is attracted to you.

~Day 2~

Cleavers grab ahold of you and seem to say, "Slow down! Take a minute here! Relax!" Imagine you are walking along and are grabbed by cleavers and you strike up a conversation. What does cleavers have to say to you?

~Day 3~

Cleavers are covered with little hooks which allow them to cling to most fabric and pet hair, leading to one of their common names, Velcro Weed. Write a poem about Velcro.

~Day 4~

Cleavers earned their name from the Old English word, *to cleave,* which means *to latch onto.* While easy to ignore as you walk by, cleavers won't let you forget them once they attach themselves to your pant leg! Write about something, someplace or someone that you want to cleave!

~Day 5~

The roots of cleavers produce a reddish dye, and can even tint bird bones if they eat the roots. Write a poem about the color red. See if you can include red tinted bird bones in your poem!

~Day 6~

Cleaver seeds can be dried and roasted to make a coffee substitute. Those that have tried it say that cleaver seed coffee tastes nearly as good as the real thing! Can you live without it or is coffee your best friend? Write an alpha poem using the letters in coffee.

~Day 7~

Amongst some hikers, cleavers are known as "backpacker colanders". A large clump of them can be used as a make-shift colander for straining pasta or rinsing berries. Do you have a backpack? Write about all of the things that you find in your backpack now. Or, write about taking a hike. Maybe make up a hiking song!

Coriander/Cilantro

The botanical name for coriander is Coriandrum sativum. When the leaves are used in their fresh form, we call this herb cilantro. The dried seeds are what we know as coriander. Coriander contains an antibacterial compound that may specifically fight against food poisoning. Coriander is thought to help lower blood sugar, blood pressure, cholesterol and can help relieve urinary tract infections.

~Day 1~

"Coriander totally overpowers every dish it touches. It's the attention-seeking brat of the food world." ~ Anonymous. Have a conversation with an attention seeking brat and write about what you learn.

~Day 2~

The fresh leaves of the coriander plant are known as cilantro. People who love cilantro say it has a refreshing, lemon/lime flavor that complements everything from guacamole to curry. It is, however, one of the few foods that elicit heated negative reactions. Those that hate the taste of cilantro say it tastes soapy, rotten or just plain disgusting. There are over 40 Facebook groups dedicated to the hatred of cilantro! So, are you a lover or a hater of cilantro! Use this line as your prompt for today – "Cilantro tastes like..........".

~Day 3~

Scientists have been able to pin down most cilantro haters as people with a shared group of olfactory-receptor genes, called OR6A2, that pick up on the smell of aldehyde chemicals. Aldehyde chemicals are found in both cilantro *and* soap. OK, so even though cilantro tastes like soap to some, soap is so wonderful! Write a thank you letter to soap.

~Day 4~

Gershon Hepner, who loves the taste, wrote a ballad which ends with this refrain:

"For me, perhaps because I'm Jewish,
it is a perfect food; like manna,
it makes me happy when I'm bluish,
and causes me to shout, "Hosanna! "
I'll always on cilantro count
in guacamole or a salad,
and since for me it's paramount,
I dedicate to it this ballad."

Write your own ballad dedicated to coriander or cilantro.

~Day 5~

"I hate you coriander

You really make me sick

The devil's arse would taste like you

If I gave it a lick." ~ Anonymous.

Write a poem for the other end of the coriander debate. "I love you, coriander,………"

~Day 6~

John Anderson wrote an alphabet poem which include these first three lines:

"**A**lphabet soup, homemade, here's how
Begin the dish with alphabet pasta and homemade chicken broth
Coriander is next, chopped finely and bruised in cloth"

Write your own alphabet poem using coriander/cilantro.

~Day 7~

In a poem titled *"Garden"* by Darren Watson, he notes:

"Apple mint and dill, Parsley and chives

Basil and coriander, Oregano and sage

The fragrances in our gardens

Stay with us all our lives."

Write about the fragrances in your garden. Or a garden that you have visited.

Cumin

The botanical name for cumin is Cuminum cyminum.
In Sanskrit, cumin is known as Jira, meaning "that
which helps digestion," and it is one of the most
mentioned herbs in the Bible. It's believed that cumin
is beneficial for heart disease, hemorrhoids,
inflammation, insomnia, vomiting, weakened
immune system and viral infections.

~Day 1~

Cumin was regarded by the Egyptians as an aphrodisiac. Write about Egyptians or aphrodisiacs!

~Day 2~

In the Middle Ages in Europe, when cumin was one of the most common spices used, it considered a symbol of love and fidelity. At a wedding, the guests would carry it in their pockets. The bride and groom, carried cumin as a sign of commitment. Capture a memory from a wedding you have attended and write about it so that anyone reading your words can visualize the scene in detail.

~Day 3~

After black pepper, cumin is the second most popular spice in the world. It is used heavily for cooking in Morocco, India, Nepal, Pakistan, Sri Lanka, Iran, Malta, Cuba, Mexico, Spain, Brazil, Turkey, Uzbekistan, Tajikistan, and China. Pick one of these countries and do a little research about it. Write about what you learned.

~Day 4~

Cumin's popularity in ancient Mesopotamia shows up in the world's oldest recipe collection, the so-called Yale Culinary Tablets, which date to about 1750 BC. Do you have an old recipe collection? If so, pick out one of your favorite recipes and write about why this is your favorite. If you do not have a collection yet, start one!

~Day 5~

A poem titled *"My Mister"*, by Rosann Fode, tells about her son learning to ride his bike. It's a story, this poem. Part of the story goes like this:

"And I want for him to slow down.

But now the training wheels have been removed

By his father when I was gone for an hour

For milk and cumin for soup.

And now he is popping the front tire

And jumping curbs

Because he is truly amazing.

And I do a great deal of breath holding,

Atheist prayers to a nonexistent God

From where I sit on the front stairs."

Write your own story about learning to ride a bike.

~Day 6~

"Once it has been introduced into a new land and culture, cumin has a way of insinuating itself deeply into the local cuisine, which is why it has become one of the most commonly used spices in the world," writes Gary Nabhan, author and researcher at the University of Arizona Southwest Center, in his recent book, *Cumin, Camels, and Caravans*. Take the perspective of cumin and write about what it is like to be so popular.

~Day 7~

In another poem titled *"Shameless"* by Melissa Schwartz, she tells a different story of a memory in an efficiency kitchenette. Part of the story goes like this:

"Curry. Cumin. Saffron.

Mmmm, the hallways always smell of spice,

her seventy-year-old body perfecting the rhythm of movement

from icebox to oven in her efficiency kitchenette.

Tangerine wall paint cracks and mixes carelessly

with bits of spice yet lingering in the air; it

follows her, this aroma that eats the eater,

dancing around her skirts

like faeries honoring their faerie queen.

She knows this, and smiles at the sliver of sun peeking through her window."

Pick any line or phrase from this poem and use it as a springboard for your writing today.

Dandelion

The botanical name for dandelion is Taraxacum officinale. The leaves made into a tea acts as a diuretic and are believed to help eliminate gall and kidney stones. Dandelion is helpful with replacing potassium. An extract of dandelion root can also be used to fight a staph infection.

~Day 1~

The dandelion root, when dried, roasted and ground like coffee, is used by some to make a coffee substitute, much like chicory root. If you love coffee like I do, write a love letter to coffee. If you are more about tea, write a love letter to dandelion tea.

~Day 2~

Each dandelion bloom is a bright golden yellow and is full of nectar. Bees love it! Beekeepers love it because it blooms from spring through late autumn, providing plenty of nectar for the buzzing bees to keep up their honey production. Write a fairy tale about bees and honey and dandelions!

~Day 3~

Here is a recipe for dandelion wine from *Mother Earth News:*

"Early in the morning when the dew is on the flowers, pick one gallon of perfect, open dandelion blossoms.

Put the flowers in a two gallon or larger open crock and pour boiling water over them. Cover the crock with cheesecloth and let it sit at room temperature for three days. Then squeeze all the juice outta the flowers, throw them away and save the liquid.

Put the liquid into a big pot and add:

3 lbs. sugar (we used brown raw sugar for healthiness but next time we'll try honey for healthierness.)

3 or 4 lemons, juice, skin, seeds, etc., all chopped up.

3 or 4 oranges, chopped

Boil mixture for 30 minutes with top on pot, cool to lukewarm, pour into crock and add 1 1/2 or 2 packages or tablespoons of yeast. Cover with cheesecloth and let brew sit for two or three weeks 'til the bubbling stops and — whammy!

Filter through cheesecloth to strain out chunks and save vitamins. Bottle."

Now, write up your own dandelion recipe. Maybe a dandelion salad? Or dandelion casserole? Or dandelion green smoothies?

~Day 4~

Dandelions have a reputation as a granter of wishes. Once the flower has gone to seed, pick it, make a wish while you are blowing the seeds out into the breeze. Make a list of your ten most precious wishes right now. Find a yard full of dandelion seed heads and have a field day!

~Day 5~

I wrote this poem some time ago titled "*Tenacious Dandelion*".

"Growing through cracks in the sidewalk, there is dandelion.

Where the endless pounding of rubber tires makes a pothole in the street,

yellow sunshine grows.

At the landfill pushing up through plastic bottles and garbage bags, dandelion smiles.

Come spring, dandelion's leaves make a healing tonic, a poor woman's brew.

Cursed as a no--good lousy weed,

dandelion transforms into a thousand seeds to delight a child."

Now, write your own poem using any line or phrase from my poem to inspire you.

~Day 6~

The dandelion flower's message seems to be "Do not give up! Even if those around you keep trying to get rid of you." Dandelion is tenacious (see my poem above) and the lesson learned by their example is to stick it out. Write about being tenacious, sticking it out, not giving up.

~Day 7~

Peter A. Gail, who wrote the book "*The Dandelion Celebration: A Guide to Unexpected Cuisine*" in 1994, recently passed away. He started the Defenders of Dandelions club, a quarterly newsletter and sponsored an annual National Dandelion Cookoff. He was known as the King of Dandelions and cultivated a patch of them in his garden. It is reported that he ate them everyday of the year, fresh or dried. As an homage to Gail, consider writing a letter to the editor of your local newspaper asking residents to defend dandelions and let them grow freely to help pollinators and humans alike!

Dill

The botanical name for dill is Anethum graveolens. Dill is thought to relieve menstrual cramps and depression, as well as, boost energy. Dill weed can repel bugs. Dill may calm an upset stomach and colicky babies.

~Day 1~

In olden days, a bride who did not want her husband to be in charge of the marriage could secretly bring dill seeds to her wedding and repeat the words "I have you, dill, Husband, when I speak, you stay still!" Write about some relationship in your life in which you wish the other person would just be quiet!

~Day 2~

Mike Judge, the creator of *"Beavis and Butt-Head,"* created the insult; "Dillweed". When he was in junior high, kids would call each other dick weed. He wanted to use it in *"Beavis and Butt-Head"*, but the TV station wouldn't allow it. So, one day he had Butt-Head call Beavis 'dill weed". It got a laugh and was cleared by the network censors. It stuck. Write about life in junior high. Or write about insults!

~Day 3~

"Nobody who is envious or ill-disposed can enter into the house if there is a sprig of dill over the door." ~ Write about a time when you were envious or ill-disposed. What happened? And then, what happened?

~Day 4~

Edward I of England, did not have enough money to repair the London Bridge, so he imposed a tax on dill and other spices that ships brought into the harbor to help raise the needed funds. Where do your tax dollars go? Make a list of 31 things that you wish your tax dollars would be used for. Then, if today is the 20th day of the month and you listed *education*, write about why *education* is important to you.

~Day 5~

Here is a method for a making dill seasoning salt. In a wide-mouthed glass jar, alternate layers of kosher salt and dill. Cover with a plastic lid and store in a dark, dry place. Allow to sit for at least two weeks. Then, empty contents of the jar into a food processor and chop lightly. Create a recipe using dill seasoning salt.

~Day 6~

In the book, *To Kill A Mockingbird* by Harper Lee, a boy by the name of Dill comes to visit in the summer. The local children, Scout and Jem are taken with Dill's imagination: "Thus we came to know Dill as a pocket Merlin, whose head teemed with eccentric plans, strange longings, and quaint fancies". Write about one of your childhood friends.

~Day 7~

Juanita Havill wrote a book titled *Heard It from Alice Zucchini: Poems About the Garden* which features fanciful odes to a variety of fruits and vegetables, including one to *"Dainty Doily Dill Weed."* Write your own ode to dill!

Echinacea

The botanical name for echinacea is Echinacea angustifolia. Health benefits of echinacea include its ability to boost the immune system, prevent cancer, cure upper respiratory problems, eliminate bacterial, yeast and viral infections, reduce inflammation, treat skin conditions, regulate blood sugar levels, treat anxiety, as well as eliminate ear infections and, in general, speed healing and recovery.

~Day 1~

An excerpt from a poem by Alice Wilde titled *Echinacea (My Mother's Garden)* reads:

"All I see is up
The pink flower stretches to forever at the sky
I stare wishing to be among the clouds
Its anterior filters the sun's warmth upon my soft arms
I sit upon the dark, sodden, summer earth
I am all to myself. Alone.
At home under their stems
So benign am I encased by the pink flower".

What would it be like to "be among the clouds"?
Write about clouds!

~Day 2~

Natasha L. Jackson wrote a poem titled *Lovely Echinacea*. Here are a few lines:

"Echinacea makes me smile.
Even though Echinacea pills are big
When you're sick, taking them is worthwhile."

Write about being sick!

~Day 3~

Alison Czeczuga wrote an article titled *4 Lessons from Our Old Friend, Echinacea* in the November, 2015 edition of the *Farm Journal*. She tells about her mother who brought herbal knowledge with her from Scotland. Here are a few of her favorite lessons about echinacea:

"Maintain graceful strength. Echinacea is a tough plant that resiliently thrives in extreme temperatures. So be like Echinacea. Embrace struggle without resentment. Stand tall and stay rooted. Find strength in being yourself, but always welcome others. Know what sustains you and make that a part of your daily life. Echinacea is constantly full of life and energy, thanks to the millions of seeds resting in its flower head. It is this cone head that allows the plant to flourish and propagate from season to season. Its instinct knows that these seeds are sacred, the source of strength and resilience. Keeping these seeds close and safe is essential. What brings you growth and sustenance? Discover your source and keep it close to you every day. Give priority to these simple rituals that bring nourishment so you can be fully present for everything life throws your way, good and bad. We are constantly evolving and changing. Embrace this. When the leaves start to drop and the seed heads turn brown, Echinacea embraces change (quite literally). So take a cue from Echinacea. Find strength in the winds of change and anticipate the new beginnings those changes bring. Seasons are short: Only put energy where it matters. A simple but powerful message from our friendly Echinacea: Put energy where it matters. Spend time with people who elevate you or find a job that expands your passions. Balance the amount of energy expended on thoughts and reactions. But, most importantly, discover the kind of energy you want in your life. Find focus and deliberation, just like Echinacea."

Whew! Great lessons, yes? I tried to whittle this down a bit, but I just think this is really good stuff. What resonates for you? Which lesson calls for you to write about it?

~Day 4~

Echinacea is also known as purple coneflower, snakeroot, black sampson, Indian head, comb flower, black susans and hedge hog. See if you can write a poem or maybe a song using one or more of these other names for echinacea.

~Day 5~

Echinacea is good example of the doctrine of signature which states that herbs resembling various parts of the body can be used to treat ailments of those body parts. The outside petals of the flowers are droopy, reminding us of how people get droopy when they have a cold or influenza. The doctrine of signatures then suggests that echinacea can be used when you are feeling droopy. Write about feeling droopy!

~Day 6~

Some people believe that if you grow echinacea around your home, it will draw prosperity to the household. What does it mean to you to be prosperous? Write an alpha poem using word prosperity.

~Day 7~

Echinacea is considered a sacred life medicines of the Navajo tribe. What do you consider to be sacred in your life? Make a list of 31 things that you cherish. If today is the 13th and you listed *Water* as number 13, write about *Water*.

Elder

The botanical name for elder is Sambucus nigra. In ancient Greece, Hippocrates, known as the "father of medicine," described elder as his "medicine chest" because of the wide array of ailments it seemed to cure. The elder plant is used for colds, the flu, sinus infections, nerve pain, inflammation, chronic fatigue, allergies, constipation and even cancer. When used within the first 48 hours of onset of symptoms, the elderberry juice extract has been found to reduce the duration of flu symptoms.

~Day 1~

In the Harry Potter books, elder is used for making magic wands. If you had a wand made from elder, write about what sort of magic would you make.

~Day 2~

Long ago, the Russians believed that elder-trees drove away evil spirits. The Bohemians used it with a spell to take away fever. The Sicilians make do with sticks of its wood will kill serpents and drive away robbers. The Serbs bring a stick of elder to their wedding ceremonies for good luck. In England, a twig of it tied into knots was carried in the pocket to prevent rheumatism. A cross made of elder and fastened to barns was supposed to keep all evil from the animals. Imagine that you get to travel back in time and visit with an elder woman from Russia, Bohemia, Sicily, Serbia or England. Write what you learn from this woman about elder.

~Day 3~

The wood of old elder trees (Elder grows like a tree in Europe, but more like a bush in America) is white and of a fine, close grain, easily cut and polishes well. It has been used for making combs, musical instruments, and toys. Write an ode to a comb, musical instrument or toy made from elder wood!

~Day 4~

The branches of the elder make wonderful flutes! Write a short children's story about marching around with a flute.

~Day 5~

Make sure that you do not eat uncooked elderberries. This is very dangerous because the seeds and for some even the leaves and branches can create a toxic reaction. Wear gloves when picking them! Write about toxic reactions, toxic poisons, toxic relationships or toxic environments!

~Day 6~

In a poem written by Jeralynn Clark titled *"Kartolfullpuffer"*, she writes about memories of her grandmother who grew elderberry bushes:

"Alone in my kitchen, snow outside my window

My heart returns to winters past, where a little girl

Stands beside Gramma, the other one...

From Germany, who grew her garden,

Vegetables and plum trees, peach trees, and pears.

Grapes on the trellis, elderberry, raspberry.

She cooked all the time, warm breads, stollen,

From the old country, her talents were keen

And she knew how to use every piece of every food

Like God gave every flower a color."

Write about your grandmother or pick a line from this poem as a prompt for your writing today.

~Day 7~

In a poem titled *"Fairy Reminiscence"*, Carol Eastman wrote these lines:

"The spring day was gorgeous so I had to go outside.

Engaging the day, I took my sewing basket and elderberry wine.

Down a path to the orchard I wound to a statuary bench as old as time.

As I was trying to sew I had trouble with a needle I was trying to thread…

When there to my rescue came an elderly fairy all dressed in red."

Hmmmm, seems like there is a theme here, elder women from long ago, grandmothers and now an elderly fairy! Pick out several words that you like from this poem and write a letter to an elderly fairy.

Fennel

The botanical name for fennel is Foeniculum vulgare. Fennel may help prevent macular degeneration. It can also help with stomach upset, bug bites, or to soothe a sore throat. Fennel is used to help maintain bone strength.

~Day 1~

Fennel has a strong smell sort of like anise or licorice. Take a deep breath and notice what you smell. Describe the smell.

~Day 2~

You can make a Catalan fish stew with fennel that is yummy! Catalonia is an area of Spain with its own distinct culture. *Seny* is a form of ancestral Catalan wisdom or sensibleness. It involves well-pondered perception of situations, level-headedness, awareness, integrity, and right action. Many Catalans consider *seny* something unique to their culture. Adopt a Catalonian philosophy and write about level-headedness or integrity or right action.

~Day 3~

"The fennel is beyond every other vegetable, delicious. It greatly resembles in appearance the largest size celery, perfectly white, and there is no vegetable equals it is flavour. It is eaten at dessert, crude, and with, or without dry salt, indeed I preferred it to every other vegetable, or to any fruit." ~ Thomas Jefferson. Write about *your* favorite fruit or vegetable.

~Day 4~

Fennel was regarded as an emblem of false flattery, as seen in Robert Greene's *"Quip for an Upstart Courtier"* (1592), "Fennell I meane for flatterers." Write a poem or a song lyric or a folk tale using both of the words, fennel and flattery.

~Day 5~

In 1842, Longfellow wrote this recommendation in his poem *"The Goblet of Life"*:

"Above the lower plants it towers,
The Fennel with its yellow flowers;
And in an earlier age than ours
Was gifted with the wondrous powers
Lost vision to restore."

Use Longfellow's words as a prompt for your writing today.

~Day 6~

The Puritans brought fennel to the "New World" to help them stay alert and ward off hunger pangs during long church services. Write about what it would be like if we eliminated hunger in the world. (Yeah, every once in a while, I like to throw in a serious topic for your journaling!)

~Day 7~

It is said that spending time around fennel will give you a "pat on the back". Write a letter to yourself from fennel giving yourself a "pat on the back"

Garlic

The botanical name for garlic is Allium sativum. Louis Pasteur scientifically determined the antibiotic qualities of garlic. Garlic is an old-time remedy for almost anything. It helps fight colds and 'flu, keeps the digestive system healthy and can act as an insect repellent.

~Day 1~

According to an Indian proverb garlic is "as good as ten mothers". Use this as your writing prompt today. If you could have ten mothers, who would you include on this list? Pick one. Write about that person.

~Day 2~

Garlic is sometimes called the "stinking rose" and there is a book by this title containing 25 poems about garlic. Write your own ode or poem to the stinking rose.

~Day 3~

Anyone who has watched tv, read horror books or been to the movies knows that garlic repels vampires. Write about vampires today before dark!

~Day 4~

A New York Yiddish saying goes: "Three nickels will get you on the subway, but garlic will get you a seat." Have you spent time in New York? On the subway? Or anywhere on a subway? Write about your experience. Or if not, write about what you can get nowadays for three nickels.

~Day 5~

"Peace and happiness, begin, geographically, where garlic is used in cooking." ~ Marcel Boulestin. Write about peace and happiness.

~Day 6~

To dream about eating garlic means you will discover hidden secrets. If you discovered hidden secrets, what would you find?

~Day 7~

In the book, *Chicken Soup for the Mothers Soul,* there is
a wonderful story titled *"Garlic Tales"* which tells
about a mother who fought the angel of death with
every sort of garlic cure including hanging bags of
garlic with camphor around the necks of her children
to ward off sore throats, diphtheria and to protect
them from polio. More about mothers! Write about
your mother.

Goldenrod

The botanical name for goldenrod is Solidago virgaurea. It is used in a traditional kidney tonic by practitioners of herbal medicine to counter inflammation and irritation caused by bacterial infections or kidney stones. Some indigenous cultures have traditionally chewed the leaves to relieve sore throats, and the roots to relieve toothaches. Goldenrod is a folk remedy for lessening bleeding and diarrhea and healing wounds.

Day 1~

Inventor Thomas Edison experimented with goldenrod to produce rubber, which it contains naturally. The tires on the Model T given to him by his friend Henry Ford were made from goldenrod. If you were inventing something made from goldenrod, what would it be? This _____ is made from goldenrod and it can be used for this and that and _____!

~Day 2~

A few lines from Celia Thaxter's poem titled "*Seaside Goldenrod*" create a beautiful image:

"Graceful, tossing plume of glowing gold,

Waving lonely on the rocky ledge;

Leaning seaward, lovely to behold,

Clinging to the high cliff's ragged edge."

Now, create your own beautiful image about goldenrod with your words.

~Day 3~

Goldenrod does NOT cause hay fever. Its pollen is too heavy to float through the air. To get hay fever, you'd have to stick a goldenrod bloom right up your nose, which would be silly. Writing about being silly. Or maybe write about your nose!

~Day 4~

The well-known naturalist who helped start our national park system, John Muir, described goldenrod in almost religious terms: "The fragrance, color, and form of the whole spiritual expression of Goldenrod are hopeful and strength-giving beyond any others I know. A single spike is sufficient to heal unbelief and melancholy." Sit down and have a conversation with goldenrod. Write about what you learn of how it provides hope and strength.

~Day 5~

A wonderful harvest time recipe calls for adding ½ cup of goldenrod flowers to your cornbread mix. Create your own recipe using goldenrod flowers.

~Day 6~

After the Boston Tea Party, when the rebellious American colonists had dumped all their tea into Boston Harbor, they discovered they had lost their favorite beverage. Not to be deterred for very long, they found that an excellent tea could be made from the leaves of the goldenrod, and they named it Liberty Tea. Write about liberty or rebellion.

~Day 7~

There are many legends about goldenrod, including this one: "Two little girls were very close friends, one was golden blond and the other was dark haired with beautiful blue eyes. They were afraid that when they grew up they might be parted from each other, so they didn't want to grow up. To solve their problem, the two little girls set out one day to visit the good witch who lived across the field far away. They came to the good witch after a long day of travel and told her of their wish to always be together. The little girls were never seen again, but whenever you see the golden yellow bloom of the goldenrod you will be sure to find the sweet blue aster always beside her." Write about one of *your* very close friends.

Ground Ivy

The botanical name for ground ivy is Glechoma Hederacea. In the earlier days, ground ivy was considered a popular remedy for coughs and headaches. The well-known herbalist, Matthew Wood recommends it be taken internally for ear aches, infections and for colds that start in the ears. Tea made from ground ivy used to treat digestive disorders, gastritis, and acid indigestion.

~Day 1~

Ground ivy possess positive energy that can be used for healing a broken heart. It´s a very protective plant. Write about healing a broken heart or how to protect your heart.

~Day 2~

In some places, ground ivy is considered a magic charm to protect cows from bad stuff. The first milking of the cows was actually done through a wreath of ground ivy. Write a short story or a poem or song lyrics using these words: magic, milk, cows, wreaths and, maybe, ground ivy!

~Day 3~

Ground ivy has a long history of beer brewing and in the British Isles, it was called *alehoff* and was used to flavor beer before the use of hops. Use the word "beer", for your writing prompt today.

~Day 4~

Ground ivy has often been used for crowns and garlands used during celebrations of Summer Solstice. Plan a Summer Solstice celebration. What will you do? Where? Who will you invite? What food will you serve? Songs to sing?

~Day 5~

This little plant is known by many names: creeping Charlie, cemetery grass, cat ivy, crow victuals, ground joy, hedgemaids, lizzy-run-up-the-hedge, run-away-robin, and wild snakeroot, amongst others. Make up your own name for ground ivy. Write a letter to ground ivy explaining why you have chosen this new name for it.

~Day 6~

Here is a fun poem and I don't know who wrote it!

"When Charlie comes a creepin'
You'll be meetin' a new friend,
And he'll be true to you, ya know,
Not kept away by winter snow:
He'll be comin' back to sow,
The seeds of friendship that will grow,
Within our hearts and keep us lively,
'Cause Creepin' Charlie, aint just any ivy!"

Write your own fun poem about Creepin Charlie!

~Day 7~

Ground ivy was recently voted on of the best plants for foraging and eating from the wild. Here is a great recipe for ground ivy tempura. "In a chilled bowl, mix together ½ cup of plain flour and ½ cup of cornmeal, 1 egg, a pinch of salt and enough water until you have a thin batter. Heat oil in a pan till it is very hot. Dip each ground ivy leaf in the batter till well coated and then fry it up! Serve with any sauce that you like."

Now, write about foraging and eating plants from the wild!

Hawthorn

The botanical name for hawthorn is Crataegus oxyacantha. Hawthorn is often called "the heart herb". It is desired for its ability to uplift and strengthen the heart both emotionally and physically. The berries of the hawthorn have been used for centuries as a natural remedy for all kinds of serious heart concerns.

~Day 1~

"Every shepherd tells his tale under the hawthorn in the dale." ~ John Milton. Make up a tale that a shepherd might tell.

~Day 2~

The hawthorn is, for many, one of the most wild, enchanted and sacred trees. Some call it the "fairy tree". There are those who make hawthorn wreaths and leave them out as gifts for the fairies in favor of good luck and prosperity. Write a very short children's story about fairies ~ a fairy tale!

~Day 3~

Hawthorn wood has been used for making small articles such as the handles for tools, boxes and combs. It makes excellent fuel and is one of the hottest burning wood known. If you were going to create something out of hawthorn wood, what would it be?

~Day 4~

As a flower essence, hawthorn helps open the heart to giving and receiving love, and can help in healing heartache. It encourages self-love and self-acceptance. Write about giving and receiving love.

~Day 5~

This beautiful, gnarled, thorny little tree can live for a very long time. It is said that if you sit by an old hawthorn tree, you can open yourself up to its wisdom. Imagine that you spend an afternoon with an old hawthorn tree. What wisdom does the hawthorn share with you? You can even write this as though you are carrying on a conversation with this old hawthorn.

~Day 6~

Folklore tells that if fishermen carry with them a thorn from the hawthorn tree, they will always have a good catch. Write a memory of sometime that you went fishing. Or if you haven't yet done so, then write about fish!

~Day 7~

In the mountains of Kentucky hawthorn is known as the thornapple tree. Locals make thornberry jelly from it because the berries are naturally very sweet. Write an alpha poem using the words "Thornberry jelly".

Horehound

The botanical name for horehound is Marrubium vulgare. Horehound is used widely to relieve coughs. It is also considered a digestive aid because it has a somewhat bitter taste that helps produce more saliva and gastric juices. It can help with motion sickness and helps to increase appetite.

~Day 1~

Horehound is a great companion plant for tomatoes. Tomatoes planted next to horehound will more happily blossom and put on fruit! OK, write about tomatoes!

~Day 2~

Horehound is said to keep off wild animals and packs of dogs if sprinkled around the home. Make a list of 31 wild animals. Then, if today is the 8th of the month and you listed *possum* for number 8 on your list of wild animals. Write about *possums* today!

~Day 3~

If you burn dried horehound leaves as incense some believe it will offer protection against any mental barriers that prevent you from reasoning wisely. Do you have any mental barriers that prevent you from reasoning wisely? Let's say it is Fear. Write a goodbye letter to Fear.

~Day 4~

Horehound's name is a derivative of Horus, the Egyptian God of sky and light. Think of as many metaphors as you can for sky and light. The sky is like _____. Light is like _____.

~Day 5~

The Dead Weather, a super rock-n-roll group, titled their debut album, *"Horehound"*. Write about your favorite rock band. Or, if you don't like rock-n-roll, write about your favorite music.

~Day 6~

My grandmother always kept a jar of horehound candy on her kitchen counter. To this day, when I remember my grandmother, I think of horehound candy. What is your favorite candy? Write a memory of a time you spent with your favorite candy.

~Day 7~

"Horehound sticks are meant to be shared with friends, don't you think?' She was dead wrong about that: Horehound sticks were meant to be gobbled down in solitary gluttony, and preferably in a locked room, but I didn't dare say so." ~ Alan Bradley. Have you ever gobbled something down in solitary gluttony? Write about what happened!

Horseradish

The botanical name for horseradish is Armoracia Rusticana. Horseradish is said to be good for getting rid of the persistent cough following influenza. If you have ever eaten too much horseradish, you know how it can clear nasal passages. Horseradish is used by some for urinary infections.

~Day 1~

"To a worm in a horseradish, the whole world is a horseradish." ~ Yiddish proverb. Write your own proverb. A proverb is a short saying stating a general truth or piece of advice.

~Day 2~

Collinsville, Illinois is known as "the horseradish capital of the world". They hold an annual festival complete with exhibits and competitions. Write a letter to the mayor of Collinsville asking him about everything there is to know about horseradish. You can simply address the letter to: Mayor, 125 S Center St, Collinsville, IL 62234. See if you get a reply!

~Day 3~

Researchers have developed a fire alarm for the deaf and hard of hearing by harnessing the strong smell of horseradish. Ally ilisothiocyanate, the oil, is extracted from the plant and used inside of the fire alarm. When the alarm is triggered by smoke, it sprays the oil into the air instead of sounding an audible alarm. Our five senses are sight, hearing, taste, smell and touch. Choose one of these senses and write about it.

~Day 4~

The comic strip *"Blondie"* often depicted Dagwood Bumstead holding towering sandwiches full of bread, lunchmeats, cheese, vegetables and usually horseradish. One of the strips shows Dagwood yelling to Blondie, "My kingdom for some horseradish!" Make a list of 31 things that you love to eat. If today is the 6th and you listed *chocolate* as the 6th thing on your list, write about your love of *chocolate*.

~Day 5~

On time on the game show Hollywood Squares, comedian George Gobel brought some laughs to the show when he was asked, "Back in the old days, when Great Grandpa put horseradish on his head, what was he trying to do?" George responded "Get it in his mouth." Write your own joke about horseradish.

~Day 6~

"I don't like purely philosophical works. I think a little philosophy should be added to life and art by way of seasoning, but to make it one's specialty seems

to me as strange as eating nothing but horseradish." ~
Boris Pasternak. Write about what you like to add to
your life as a way of seasoning it. Or write about the
seasons of your life?

~Day 7~

"If you need warmth
It's better to go to the snow-bound garden.
In the farthest corner you'll find
The lonely hut of the horseradish.
Yes, it's here, the poor hut of a horseradish.
Is there a light on inside? — Yes, he's always at home.
Knock at the door of horseradish.
Knock on the door of his hut.
Knock, he will let you in."

~from a poem, *SONG 352,* by Oleh Lysheha.

Imagine that you are visiting the poor, lonely hut
where Horseradish lives. Describe this place in detail
and tell about your visit with Horseradish.

Hyssop

The botanical name for hyssop is Hyssopus officinalis. Hyssop can work as a remedy for sore throats. It fights infections and parasites! It is one of the great home remedies for acne and hemorrhoids.

~Day 1~

So strong is the scent of hyssop that at one time women pressed it into their psalm books to keep themselves from falling asleep during church services. Have you ever fallen asleep in an awkward place or time? I fell asleep once in an airport and missed my flight. Write about nodding off at the wrong time or the wrong place.

~Day 2~

Hyssop is mentioned many times in the *Bible*. Perhaps the best-known verse is in *Psalm 51*, where it states, "Thou shalt purge me with hyssop, and I shall be clean." The name comes from the Greek word *hyssopos* and the Hebrew word for *Azob*, a holy herb, used for cleaning sacred places. Are there any places that you consider to be sacred in your life? Write a letter of thanks for this sacred space. It could be a temple, or a mountain top, or a synagogue or a church or a river, for example. Or maybe your kitchen table!

~Day 3~

It has also been left at grave sites to protect the dead. Have you ever visited the grave of a dearly departed one? Write about any traditions you have related to graveyards. Or, if you don't engage in such practice, then just write about graveyards.

~Day 4~

It's not a surprise, given the historical use of hyssop for purification and cleansing, that it can be found as a lovely ingredient in homemade lye soap! Capture a special moment in your life involving soap! Describe it in detail almost as though you have taken a photo of the moment with words.

~Day 5~

"If you can use the word *hyssop* seven times in a single poem you can do anything." ~ Rick Lupert. Write a poem using the word hyssop seven times!

~Day 6~

It is thought that carrying hyssop in your pocket will prevent unkind thoughts and energy from sticking to you. What do you carry in your pockets? Or your purse? Make a list of things you usually carry in your pocket, then, close your eyes, and point your finger at the list. Write about the item that your finger has chosen.

~Day 7~

Emily Pfeiffer's long and inspiring poem titled *"Blown Seed of Song"* contains this reference to hyssop:

"But like the hyssop where it grows-

Its rootlets biting on the stone-

It learns how life may best sustain

Itself, how turn each outward wrong

To inward profiting of pain…"

Pick any line from this poem and use it for your writing prompt today.

Juniper

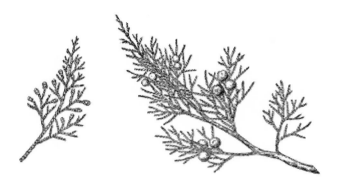

The botanical name for juniper is Juniperus communis. Juniper berry essential oil is commonly used for sore throat, respiratory infections, fatigue, muscle aches and arthritis. It can also help relieve skin rashes, boost the immune system, help with insomnia and improve digestion.

~Day 1~

In the 1500s, a Dutch pharmacist created an inexpensive diuretic using the juniper berry and called it gin. Gin comes from the Dutch word for juniper which is *jenever*. The drink caught on as more than a medicine and today juniper berry is still giving gin its distinctive flavor. Write about your favorite alcoholic beverage. Maybe a bawdy bar room song? Or, if you don't drink booze, write about *your* favorite beverage. Maybe some sort of silly song for a picnic?

~Day 2~

In a poem titled *Juniper Dryad,* Natalie writes (in part)....

"At dawn, her unripe berries glint a bluish milky white —
Pale ova, pure in their infancy;
The lustrous pearls nest
In nooks between several sprigged
Fingers; and her hardy skin
Seeps rich with olfactory bliss — sweet
Sweat of gin, balsamic breath
Of damp, green wood."

A dryad is a tree nymph or tree spirit in Greek mythology. Write your own poem, or song, or story about a juniper dryad.

~Day 3~

There is a poetry journal with the title *Juniper.* You can find their website online at

https://juniperpoetry.com/

They take submissions several times a year. Send in one of your poems!

~Day 4~

"The fire. The odor of burning juniper is the sweetest fragrance on the face of the earth, in my honest judgment; I doubt if all the smoking censers of Dante's paradise could equal it. One breath of juniper smoke, like the perfume of sagebrush after rain, evokes in magical catalysis, like certain music, the space and light and clarity and piercing strangeness of the American West. Long may it burn." ~ Edward Abbey.

Write a poem using "the sweetest fragrance on the face of the earth" as the first line. Then, the second line will have 8 words. The third line, 7 words and so on until the last line has just one word, juniper.

~Day 5~

"If a man knew enough, he could write a whole book about the juniper tree." ~ Edward Abbey. If you could write a whole book, what would you write about? Maybe write the first paragraph?

~Day 6~

In a poem titled *Juniper and Bone,* Dennis Lee lists many things he would like to learn from his momma. Here are a few of the lines including the one which mentions juniper:

"Old momma teach me moonlight
    Old momma teach me skin
And momma teach me heartland
    And teach me highway fear
Old momma teach me nerve ends
    Made of juniper and bone"

Write a poem, following this style, listing what you would like to learn from your momma.

~Day 7~

M.P. Kozlowsky wrote a book titled *Juniper Berry*, which is the name of the main character. Here is a scene from the story where Juniper spends some time in a study full of books:

"But for Juniper, the very best thing about the study was the smell. She reveled in the delightful scent wafting through the stuffy air. It was what first drew her into the room. She followed her nose down the hall, and it wasn't long before she realized it was the pages of the books that so tickled her fancy and sense of smell. She grabbed a book from off the shelves, opened the spine — hoping to hear a crack — and inhaled deeply. Then she grabbed another and another. She decided that whichever book smelled best that day, and every day after, she'd read — typically the older the better."

Write about a memory you have of spending time with books.

Lavender

The botanical name for English lavender is Lavandula officinalis. Many people benefit from lavender essential oils to reduce anxiety and stress, to improve brain functioning, to help heal burns and wounds, to improve sleep, to relieve pain and headaches.

~Day 1~

The word lavender comes from the Latin *lavandus* "to be washed," or *lavare,* "to wash." In medieval times, the washing women were known as "lavenders". They used lavender to scent drawers and dried their laundry on lavender bushes. Maybe write a song today that you could sing when you are doing your laundry?

~Day 2~

"It always seems to me as if the lavender was a little woman in a green dress, with a lavender bonnet and a white kerchief. She's one of those strong, sweet, wholesome people, who always rest you, and her sweetness lingers long after she goes away." ~ Myrtle Reed . Write about someone you know who is strong, sweet, wholesome and their sweetness lingers long.

~Day 3~

"There's an old story about the beautiful fairy called Lavandula who was born in the wild lavender of the mountains. She grew up and wandered away from the mountain, looking for a new place to make her home. One day she came across the stony, barren, uncultivated landscape. This made her so sad she cried hot tears- that fell into the ground and stained it a lovely lavender color. And that is where, forever more, the lavender of her birthplace began to grow." ~ Deborah Lawrenson, from a book titled *"The Sea Garden"*. If you were searching for a new place to make your home, where would it be and what herbs might you plant there? Or, if you are perfectly content where you are now, write about your home.

~Day 4~

Throughout history lavender has symbolized love, affection, cleanliness, purity, chastity, protection, longevity, acknowledgement, perseverance and peace. Pick any one of these virtues and write a character sketch. For example, if you choose longevity. Write about what it would be like if you met Longevity at a potluck. What would Longevity look like? What would it be like to have a conversation with Longevity? Would Longevity be wearing a lavender scent? What food would Longevity bring to the potluck?

~Day 5~

Lavender is, by legend, a spiritually rejuvenating herb that relaxes your mind and quiets the ego voice. It is often used as an aromatherapy before a meditation. It is believed to enhance the vibrations of your third-eye chakra—which can strengthen insights. Lavender is thought to deepen spiritual understanding. Close your eyes and let your thoughts wander. Ask for wisdom from lavender. See if you come across any new insights about your life. Quick! Write it down!

~Day 6~

In the beginning of a poem titled *"The Third Mist"* by Anthony Sloasin, he equates love with a lavender mist:

"Love is a lavender mist

loosening sealed windows

gliding through key holes of bolted doors

melting frost from the heart

placing it in a nest of warmth

where a chorus of miracles lie."

Use this as your writing prompt today. Maybe write about love?

~Day 7~

"Avoid men who call you Baby, and women who have no friends, and dogs that scratch at their bellies and refuse to lie down at your feet. Wear dark glasses; bathe with lavender oil and cool fresh water. Seek shelter from the sun at noon." ~ Alice Hoffman . What advice do you have to offer?

Lemon Balm

The botanical name for balm is *Melissa officinalis.* It is also known as sweet balm, lemon balm, or honey plant. Not to be confused with bee balm or monarda which is an entirely different herb. Lemon balm is said to be useful against colds, fevers, and influenza. It has also been used against sleep disorders, nervous stomachs, migraine, and depression.

~Day 1~

Lemon balm has been referred to as "the elixir of life". An elixir is a magical potion. If you were creating your own elixir for life, what would you use? Write up your recipe.

~Day 2~

Lemon balm attracts bees. We now know that bees are in danger due to the use of pesticides. Many people have taken up beekeeping as a way to extend protection for precious bees. Here is a haiku I wrote about bees and lemon balm:

"Lemon Balm is loved
The bees sing and dance all day
I sit and drink tea"

Write your own haiku about lemon balm or bees or both! Haiku is a traditional form of Japanese poetry. Haiku poems consist of 3 lines. The first and last lines of a Haiku have 5 syllables and the middle line has 7 syllables. The lines rarely rhyme.

~Day 3~

John Hussey, of Sydenham, who lived to the age of 116, breakfasted for fifty years on balm tea sweetened with honey. Would you like to live till the age of 116? Why or why not? What do you imagine life would be like for you if you live this long. Write a letter to your 116 year old self.

~Day 4~

In a poem titled *"Nectarines"* by Bernadette Geyer, she shares the lines:

"The afternoon is surreal with lemon balm and lotus blossoms,
punctuated with a too-distinct clarity of tangled Kudzu,
and you in a hammock."

Imagine a lovely afternoon. Imagine that lemon balm was a part of the loveliness of your day. Use the lines from this poem as a springboard for your writing today.

~Day 5~

In several of Shakespeare's plays, he speaks of lemon balm as a comfort for grief reflecting the common understanding of those times. Grief is difficult to write about, isn't it? And yet, it is really a regular part of life. Make a word map with grief at the center of the page. Draw lines out from the word grief including words that come to mind when you think of grief. You might then choose one of the words you associate with grief and write about it.

~Day 6~

According to an old Arabian proverb, "Balm makes the heart merry and joyful." What else makes your heart merry and joyful? Write about it.

~Day 7~

In the Victorian language of flowers, lemon balm could be added to a tussie mussie or floral bouquet to signify "pleasant company of friends," or "memories". Write about a memory you have of spending time in the pleasant company of friends.

Linden

The botanical name for linden is Tilia americana. In Europe, it is often called a lime tree. It is also sometimes called basswood. Linden flower tea is often used in healing many illnesses, especially cough, colds, fever, headache, inflammation, infections, high blood pressure and as a diuretic and sedative.

~Day 1~

"The Linden Avenue" poem by Boris Pasternak is long and lovely. I just had to include the entire piece:

"Here, with their crowns each other hiding,
Enormous linden trees engage
In dusky, quiet celebration
Of their two hundred years of age.
And underneath their vaulted branches,
Across the regularly drawn
Symmetric avenues, grow flowers
In flower-beds upon a lawn.

Beneath the trees, on sandy pathways,
Not one bright spot relieves the dark,
Save-like an opening in a tunnel-
The distant entrance of the park.

But now the blossom-time is starting,
The walled-in linden trees reveal
And spread about within their shadow
Their irresistible appeal.
The visitors, in summer clothing,
While walking on the crunchy sand,
Breathe in unfathomable fragrance
Which only bees can understand.

This gripping scent is theme and subject,
Whereas-however well they look-
The flower-beds, the lawn, the garden,
Are but the cover of a book.
The clustered, wax-bespattered flowers

On massive trees, sedate and old,
Lit up by raindrops, burn and sparkle
Above the mansion they enfold. "

Pick a line and use it as your writing prompt today.

~Day 2~

"The garden was alive with birdsong. A blackbird looked at her with a cheeky eye, then hopped away to search for worms. The scent of the linden blossoms was intoxicating." ~ Kate Forsyth, from *The Wild Girl*. Write about intoxicating scents!

~Day 3~

Lindens can grow 130 feet tall and live on average 500 years. A linden tree at the Westonbirt Arboretum in Gloucestershire, England is said to be 2,000 years old. Fossils of linden leaves from over 70 million years ago were found in Northern Siberia. Write about what life might have been like 500 or 2000 or 70 million years ago!

~Day 4~

The linden tree figures in history and folklore across
Europe. In Slavic mythology, the linden was
considered a sacred tree. In Estonia and Lithuania,
women conducted rituals in front of linden trees,
asking for fertility and tranquility. In Germany,
judicial cases were often tried under the tree as it was
said to inspire fairness and justice. Create a ritual to
use under the linden tree to insure fertility, tranquility
or justice.

~Day 5~

Another example of the importance of the linden in
German culture is this verse by Wilhelm Müller, *der
Lindenbaum*, one of the two dozen poems of *Die
Winterreise*, the cycle set to music by Franz Schubert:

"By the fountain, near the gate,
There stands a linden tree;
I have dreamt in its shadows
so many sweet dreams.
I carved on its bark
so many loving words;
I was always drawn to it,

whether in joy or in sorrow.

Today again I had to pass it
in the dead of night.
And even in the darkness
I had to close my eyes.
Its branches rustled
as if calling to me:
"Come here, to me, friend,
Here you will find your peace!"
The frigid wind blew
straight in my face,
my hat flew from my head,
I did not turn back.

Now I am many hours
away from that spot
and still I hear the rustling:
"There you would have found peace!"

If you were walking by a linden tree with rustling
branches, what would it be calling to you? What does
linden want you to know?

~Day 6~

In Poland, too, the linden is a highly cherished tree, at the heart of many Polish legends. In Polish, the month of July, *Lipiec'*, is named for *lipa'*, the Polish word for the linden tree. According to Polish legend an old linden tree should never be cut down: as this would result in great misfortunes for the community. Today in Poland it's common to see roadside shrines under a linden tree. The tree is believed to be favorite of the Virgin Mary and prayers offered under it are considered to have a good chance of being answered. Write a prayer that you might leave under a linden tree the next time you happen upon one when you are out and about.

~Day 7~

Carl Linnaeus, the father of modern taxonomy (the standardized method by which we name all living organisms) greatly admired the linden tree, because he adopted the Latin derivation of linden as his surname. If you were going to adopt a new name for yourself, what would it be and what does this mean for you?

Mint

The botanical name for spearmint is Mentha viridis. The botanical name for peppermint is Mentha piperita. There are an incredible variety of mints to enjoy! Mint is known to improve digestion, relieve cold symptoms, help with oral hygiene and give a boost to brain functioning.

~Day 1~

"I come from down south, where vegetation does not know its place. Honeysuckle can work through cracks in your walls and strangle you while you sleep. Kudzu can completely shroud a house and a car parked in the yard in one growing season. Wisteria can lift a building off its foundation, and certain terrifying mints spread so rapidly that just the thought of them on a summer night can make your hair stand on end. " ~ Bailey White . Have you ever been terrified by a plant? Write about any scary encounters you have had with vegetation!

~Day 2~

Ed Morris' poem titled *Ice Cream* is yummy! Here is a bite of the poem:

"I think that I shall never dream
A poem lovely as ice cream.
It's soft and smooth and cold and sweet—
An opulent delight to eat.
Vanilla, chocolate, cookie dough,
Pecan, or mint—my heart's aglow."

Write a poem about ice cream. Is mint flavored ice cream your favorite?

~Day 3~

Mice do not like the smell of mint, either fresh or dried. They any place where it is scattered. I wrote a poem some years ago titled *Mice Infestations and the Smell of Freshly Baked Bread.* Here are a few lines:

"The cabin smells faintly of mice.

Do you know this?

The smell of mice infestations?

It's the smell of my grandmother's house, musty, moldy with mice droppings along the baseboards.

The drawer in her china cabinet was full of root beer barrels, licorice, chocolate fudge, and yes, a few mice turds.

I never cared.

I would pull out a peppermint and sit, eyes wide open while Grandma taught me how to read tea leaves and whispered my future."

Write about mice infestations or grab any other line from my poem to inspire you!

~Day 4~

"Encouragement is like a chocolate mint its taste so divinely sweet." ~ Bobby May. Write a character sketch about Encouragement. If you met Encouragement, what would you talk about?

~Day 5~

"I want you to take a sleeve of Thin Mints and line them up on the edge of the kitchen counter and when I'm hungry I can just bend over and sweep a cookie into my mouth like I'm scoring a goal in hockey. " ~ Jack Gantos . My daughter's favorite Girl Scout cookie is also Thin Mints. Now that you've written about your favorite ice cream, take some time today to write about your favorite cookies! Maybe a story about a moment in your life involving cookies?

~Day 6~

"The yard was full of tomato plants about to ripen, and mint, mint, everything smelling of mint, and one fine old tree that I loved to sit under on those cool perfect starry California October nights unmatched anywhere in the world. " ~ Jack Kerouac. Write about a cool, perfect, starry October night.

~Day 7~

"She wanted to hold foreign syllables like mints on her tongue until they dissolved into fluency." ~ Anthony Marra . Have you tried learning another language? I am studying Spanish right now. Write about foreign syllables. Maybe see if you can write something short in another language? Maybe about mint? In Spanish, the word for mint is *menta*.

Monarda

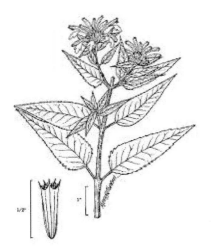

The botanical name for monarda is Monarda didyma. Monarda is also known as bee balm and wild bergamot. Native Americans have used monarda as an antiseptic for skin infections and minor wounds. It has been used for stomach and bronchial ailments. Crushed and boiled monarda leaves are used to treat headache and fever.

~Day 1~

Monarch butterflies and hummingbirds especially enjoy monarda. Write a conversation between the butterfly and the bird about the pleasures they find with this herb.

~Day 2~

The plant was named for the Spanish botanist Nicholas Monardes, who wrote a book in 1574 describing plants of North America. If you could have a plant named after you, which one would it be? And what would it be called? What is special about this particular plant for you?

~Day 3~

"Aunt Bett sure knew a lot and I believed everything she said. We gathered bee balm for food and medicinal purposes, though I secretly knew that Aunt Bett brewed it into a tea which she drank every night. She told me it calmed the bees, and if it calmed the bees, then surely it would keep her calm. Maybe so, because I never saw Aunt Bett in a tizzy over anything." ~ Sharon Brown. Write about what you do to calm yourself and keep from having a tizzy over anything!

~Day 4~

Monarda symbolizes money and prosperity. It is thought to protect from evil and illness. It is also said to represent fertility and promote restful sleep. See if you can write a bit of prose using all of the following words: money, prosperity, evil, illness, fertility and restful sleep. Aaah, go ahead! Try it!

~Day 5~

Daniel Turner references monarda (or bee balm) in a poem titled *"What Tomorrow Will Bring"*. Here is an excerpt from the poem:

"My lungs filled with fresh morning air
Hummingbirds humming over red bee balm
A moment for silent prayer
Tomorrow brings the blue bird's song"

Pick a line from this verse and use it as a springboard for your writing today.

~Day 6~

"The mullein had finished blooming, and stood up out of the pastures like dusty candelabra. The flowers of Queen Anne's lace had curled up into birds' nests, and the bee balm was covered with little crown-shaped pods. In another month -- no, two, maybe -- would come the season of the skeletons, when all that was left of the weeds was their brittle architecture." ~ Elizabeth Enright. This writer uses simile here to paint a picture of a garden dying, drying up after first frost. Create your own picture of a garden using simile. The garden is like _____.

~Day 7~

Monarda is also called Oswego Tea. Native Americans from the Iroquois Nation who came from a place called Oswego showed the Colonists how to make tea from the plant after the Boston tea party in 1773. See what you can discover about the Iroquois Nation and write about what you learn.

Mullein

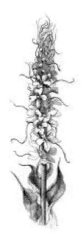

The botanical name for mullein is Verbascum Thapsus. Mullein has been used as medicine since ancient times for inflammation, diarrhea, coughs and other lung-related ailments. An oil made from the flowers is often used to treat earaches. In Appalachia, mullein is used for bruises, and burns.

~Day 1~

Mullein is also known as Torches, Our Lady's Flannel, Blanket Herb, Velvet Plant, Woollen, Candlewick Plant, Shepherd's Staff, Beggar's Stalk, Hare's Beard, Old Man's Flannel and Hag's Taper. Pick one of these names and use it for a 5-minute writing sprint.

~Day 2~

"It has a moistening, lubricating effect on the synovial membranes… so that it is hydrating to the spine and joints. It is often indicated in back injuries. People think they are untreatable and incurable, but an increase the synovial fluids will make the spine more pliable and comfortable. The vertebra will slip back into place more readily, pain and inflammation will decrease and the condition will get better." ~ Matthew Wood's information about mullein from his *Book of Herbal Wisdom.* Write about your spine!

~Day 3~

In Louisa May Alcott's *Little Men*, Demi comments, "I know one thing about this mullein leaf: the fairies use them for blankets." Write about a favorite blanket.

~Day 4~

The name mullein may be from *mollis*, Latin for soft, a description of the big hairy leaves. Write the word "Soft" in the middle of your page and draw a circle around it. Write down the words that you associate with the word soft. You will create a clustering of words about being soft or things that are soft. Take a few minutes and reflect on the collection of words you have written. Now, begin free writing with these words and see where the writing takes you!

~Day 5~

And then, there are the stories of mullein use as "Cowboy's Toilet Paper." Be advised that if you are out roughing it, camping maybe, and use mullein for TP or a wash cloth, be certain to wipe with the flow of the hairs not against! Write about going camping or hiking and making do with what you find in the wild. Or write about toilet paper!

~Day 6~

Back in the day, Quaker women weren't allowed to wear make-up, so these clever ladies rubbed the hairy leaves of mullein on their cheeks to make a homemade blush. Mullein was known as Quaker's Rouge. What about make-up? Do you love it or leave it alone? Write about your life with or without lipstick, mascara, eye liner, eye shadow, or blush.

~Day 7~

The Mullein Meadow by Jean Blewett (1872 - 1934)

"Down in the mullein meadow

The lusty thistle springs,

The butterflies go criss-cross,

The lonesome catbird sings,

The alderbush is flaunting

Her blossoms white as snow--

The same old mullein meadow

We played in long ago.

The waste land of the homestead,

The arid sandy spot,

Where reaper's song is never heard,

Where wealth is never sought,

But where the sunshine lingers,

And merry breezes come

To gather pungent perfumes

From the mullein-stalks a-bloom.

There's a playground on the hillside,

A playhouse in the glade,

With mulleins for a garden,

And mulleins for a shade.

And still the farmer grumbles

That nothing good will grow

In this old mullein meadow

We played in long ago!"

Write about growing in tough places.

Mugwort

The botanical name for mugwort is Artemisia vulgaris. It is a natural bug repellant. The plant can help to alleviate digestive and intestinal issues like ulcers, vomiting, nausea and constipation. Mugwort should never be used internally during pregnancy or lactation as it can cause uterine contractions and can be passed through the breast milk.

~Day 1~

Mugwort relieves sore feet just by placing the leaves inside the shoes. Write about about sore feet or shoes!

~Day 2~

Mugwort is named for Artemis, the Greek goddess of the moon, wild animals and hunting. Write an Ode to Artemis!

~Day 3~

Mugwort is often used as one of the main ingredients in sleep pillows, and it said to bring the dreamer more lucid dreams. Write about a dream you have had recently.

~Day 4~

"I used to walk one particular route to work that always led me past a population of mugwort. It was an unpleasant and ugly stretch to walk through, full of trash and city grime, but the mugwort always provided a glimpse of beauty and grace with its silvery green glow. It felt like the mugwort was welcoming me to my new city, and whispered to me an important reminder: that I could find beauty wherever I looked for it." ~ Steph Zabel. Write about finding beauty wherever you look for it.

~Day 5~

Every flower is associated with certain virtues or qualities. Mugwort flowers symbolize happiness and good luck. Imagine that Happiness and Good Luck ran into each other at the local coffee shop. Write about their conversation.

~Day 6~

You can make a really yummy soup using mugwort, potatoes, cream, chicken (or vegetable broth), mushrooms, onions and garlic. Write a soup memory. Once upon a time, soup......

~Day 7~

Burning herbs or smudging to "clear the energy" does just that. Science now knows that this actually kills bad bacteria lingering around. Mugwort is antimicrobial which makes for a great incense or smudge. Write about what you do to "clear the energy" around you or within you.

Mustard

The botanical name for black mustard is Brassica nigra. Mustard greens are great for cleansing the liver. They're high in plant chlorophyll, so mustard greens can literally pull environmental toxins from the bloodstream. Mustard greens may help to lower cholesterol.

~Day 1~

"Almost anything is edible with a dab of French mustard on it." ~ Nigel Slater. Do you love mustard on your food? Or, do you prefer other condiments? Write a short children's story about condiments.

~Day 2~

"I never lose an opportunity of urging a practical beginning, however small, for it is wonderful how often in such matters the mustard-seed germinates and roots itself." ~ Florence Nightingale. Write about small beginnings that germinate and grow.

~Day 3~

"There are many reasons to celebrate, but National Mustard Day is just ridiculous." ~ Lily O'Brien. What ridiculous traditions can you create to celebrate National Mustard Day?

~Day 4~

"I had forgotten what mustard fields looked like... Sheet upon sheet of blazing yellow, half way between sulphur and celandine, with hot golden sunshine pouring down upon them out of a dazzling June sky. It thrilled me like music." ~ Monica Baldwin. Write about what thrills you.

~Day 5~

"A tale without love is like beef without mustard: insipid." ~ Anatole France. Write a love story or love song or a poem about love.

~Day 6~

"Feelings, whether of compassion or irritation, should be welcomed, recognized, and treated on an absolutely equal basis; because both are ourselves. The tangerine I am eating is me. The mustard greens I am planting are me. I plant with all my heart and mind. I clean this teapot with the kind of attention I would have were I giving the baby Buddha or Jesus a bath. Nothing should be treated more carefully than anything else. In mindfulness, compassion, irritation, mustard green plant, and teapot are all sacred. " ~ Nhat Hanh. Choose a line from this message and write a response. Where do these thoughts of Thich Nhat Hanh take you?

~Day 7~

"Hitting a golf ball correctly is the most sophisticated and complicated maneuver in all of sports, with the possible exception of eating a hot dog at a ball game without getting mustard on your shirt. " ~ Ray Fitzgerald . Write about golf or baseball or how to keep from getting mustard on your shirt.

Nettle

The botanical name for nettle is Urtica urens. The plant has been used for centuries as a diuretic and for treating painful muscles and joints, eczema, arthritis, gout, and anemia. Nettle is also said to stimulate hair growth, prevent diarrhea, heal wounds, and provide relief from asthma.

~Day 1~

This herb is commonly known as stinging nettle! It is reported by many that the juice of the nettle proves an antidote for its own sting. The juice of the dock, which is often found growing nearby nettle, has the same beneficial action. An old rhyme goes like this:

'Nettle in, dock out.
Dock rub nettle out!'

Now, write your own rhyme about nettle.

~Day 2~

"Nature is imperfectly perfect, filled with loose parts and possibilities, with mud and dust, nettles and sky, transcendent hands-on moments and skinned knees." ~ Richard Louv. Write about the perfect imperfection of nature or of life!

~Day 3~

"In Scotland, I have eaten nettles, I have slept in nettle sheets, and I have dined off a nettle tablecloth. The young and tender nettle is an excellent potherb. The stalks of the old nettle are as good as flax for making cloth. I have heard my mother say that she thought nettle cloth more durable than any other species of linen." ~ Thomas Campbell. If you could have a nice bolt of nettle cloth, what would you make out of it?

~Day 4~

Here is the first verse of a poem titled *Stinging Nettle* by Janaki Nilmini:

"The first among to wake up in the Spring
The award winner, comes with a sting
Cannot touch the super herbal queen
Stinging Nettle pubescent and green"

Close your eyes and point your finger at this bit of poetry. If your finger lands on the word "sting", write a poem using the word "sting"!

~Day 5~

"With a tiny bit of effort, the nettle would be useful; if you neglect it, it becomes a pest. So then we kill it. How many men are like nettles My friends, there is no such thing as a weed and no such thing as a bad man. There are only bad cultivators." ~ Victor Hugo. Some think of nettles as a nasty weed that causes pain and should be eradicated. Yet, we know that it has great value. Write about some experience which caused you pain, but ended up being of value.

~Day 6~

"It's difficult to show a nettle much love. You can't touch it, for one thing. For many children the stinging pain of their first nettle rash is also a gentle first lesson about the darker side of nature. We *told* you not to go charging into the bushes after that football."
~ Zoe Kleinman. Tell one of the first lessons you learned about nature as a child.

~Day 7~

In the fairy tale of *The Wild Swans* by Hans Christian Andersen, a young girl's brothers have been turned into swans by their evil stepmother. A kindly fairy instructs her to gather nettles by night, spin their fibers into a prickly green yarn, and knit the yarn into a coat for each swan brother in order to break the spell -- all of which she must do without speaking a word or her brothers will die. The nettles sting her hands, but she works, until the nettle coats are almost done. She runs out of time before she can finish the sleeve on the very last coat. She flings the coats onto her swan-brothers and they transform back into young men. The youngest brothers, the one with the incomplete coat is left with a wing in the place of one arm. Now, write your own fairy tale about nettles.

Onion

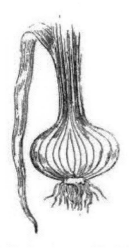

The botanical name for onion is Allium cepa. A number of studies suggest that onions help reduce the risk of developing colon, ovarian and mouth cancers. According to the National Arthritis Foundation, quercetin found in onions may be especially beneficial for arthritis because it helps to reduce inflammation. In Russia, people will put pieces of onion in their nostrils to relieve a cold.

~Day 1~

"Life is an onion - you peel it year by year and sometimes cry." ~ Carl Sandburg. Use this line to inspire your writing today.

~Day 2~

"Writers are like onions, layers upon layers upon layers." ~ Luke Taylor. Write about writers! Or create another simile, "Writers are like_____".

~Day 3~

"An onion can make people cry but there's never been a vegetable that can make people laugh." ~ Will Rogers . Write some jokes about vegetables that will make people laugh.

~Day 4~

"It is hard to imagine a civilization without onions." ~ Julia Child. Write a short story about life without onions. Or create an imaginary civilization in which onions play an important part or maybe where onions are illegal?

~Day 5~

"This is every cook's opinion -
no savory dish without an onion,
but lest your kissing should be spoiled
your onions must be fully boiled." ~ Jonathan Swift .

Write a rhyming poem about onions or kissing!

~Day 6~

"In onion is strength; and a garden without it lacks flavour. The onion, in its satin wrappings, is among the most beautiful of vegetables; and it is the only one that represents the essence of things. It can almost be said to have a soul." ~ Charles Dudley Warner. I grew up in St. Louis on soul music. Write a song about the soul of the onion! Or maybe write a list of 31 essential people, places or things in your life. If today is the 22nd day of the month and you listed *socks* as number 22 on your list, write about *socks*.

~Day 7~

"It's toughest to forgive ourselves. So, it's probably best to start with other people. It's almost like peeling an onion. Layer by layer, forgiving others, you really do get to the point where you can forgive yourself." ~ Patty Duke. Imagine that you end up sitting next to Forgiveness on the bus. What would you ask of Forgiveness? Write about your conversation with Forgiveness.

Oregano

The botanical name for oregano is Origanum vulgare. Oregano essential oil can help manage athlete's foot or toenail fungus, common colds, infection, gingivitis, earaches, and digestive problems such as heartburn.

~Day 1~

The name of this plant comes from the Greek word for mountains which is *oreos* and the Greek word for joy which is *ganeos*. Oregano was commonly called "joy of the mountains" due to its beauty and abundance. Write a conversation with a mountain.

~Day 2~

In 1953, Dean Martin sang with gusto, "When the moon hits your eye like a bigga pizza pie / That's *amore!*" Ever since, the love affair between pizza, oregano and America has steadily grown. Americans consume more than 14 million pounds of oregano every year. Oregano is the number one herb imported to the U.S. Write a modern love (*amore*) song for pizza. Be sure to mention oregano!

~Day 3~

Oregano is sometimes called the "prince of herbs". If oregano is the prince of herbs, which herbs make up the rest of the royal family? Write a ballad about the herbal royal family.

~Day 4~

The ancient Greeks believed that oregano was the herb of Aphrodite, the goddess of love, who is said to have created it as the herb of joy for her garden. Write about joy!

~Day 5~

The first line in a poem titled "*Oregano*" by Myke Leas goes: "Oregano draws out infection, my heart draws out your lies". Where do your words go after reading this line?

~Day 6~

"Someone sits beside me, bringing with him the smell of cigarettes and oregano in a pleasant sort of way." From a poem titled "*Oregano Cigaretts*" by Shayne M. Phillips. Think about a time when someone sitting next to you smelled in a pleasant sort of way. Capture that moment in detail. Like a photograph using words.

~Day 7~

"I know a woman who insists that she can cook only from a recipe. She measures everything precisely. To her, a half-teaspoon of oregano means exactly that. To me, a half-teaspoon of oregano is hardly worth putting in a sauce or salad dressing. I shake a small mound of the dried herb into my palm, sprinkle it in with other ingredients, stir, taste, smell, and either leave it or pinch in more." ~ Sylvia Levinson. What sort of a cook are you? How do you approach cooking? With precision, by the book? Or by the handful and a pinch? Or do you avoid it entirely? Write about cooking.

Parsley

The botanical name for parsley is Petroselinum crispum. Parsley is thought to be beneficial for heart and brain health. It is considered an antibacterial and an antifungal. It relieves constipation.

~Day 1~

"It turns out that, at social gatherings, as a source of entertainment, conviviality, and good fun, I rank somewhere between a sprig of parsley and a single ice-skate." ~ Dorothy Parker. Use this as a springboard for your writing today. "At social gatherings, I................"

~Day 2~

"If you who are reading this are studying herbal medicine or just have your own reasons to want to know this herb at a much deeper level than usual then I urge you to take a dose of the tincture or a good amount (i.e. a cup) of the tea and then, with a quiet and attentive mind, observe for yourself how you feel the 'action' of the herb. Apart from all the intense greeny goodness (and of course strong tastes!) you will certainly feel I think you also may very well be able to notice how Parsley gets right inside the 'fluids' of the body - its kind of like a gentle bottle brush that cleans out the pipes! However much you feel the Parsley on arrival I think that, so long as you are open to it, you will also certainly notice its exit. 'Peeing like a racehorse' is one phrase that came to my mind!" ~ Richard Whelan. What phrase comes to mind for you when you think of parsley?

~Day 3~

"If a parsley farmer is sued, can they garnish his wages? " ~ George Carlin. Funny stuff! Write your own joke about parsley.

~Day 4~

"Pounding fragrant things - particularly garlic, basil, parsley - is a tremendous antidote to depression. But it applies also to juniper berries, coriander seeds and the grilled fruits of the chilli pepper. Pounding these things produces an alteration in one's being - from sighing with fatigue to inhaling with pleasure." ~ Patience Gray. Have you ever been depressed? What did you do to alter your mood? Take this line and go with it, "Pounding fragrant things, ..."

~Day 5~

On October 2, 1937, the dictator of the Dominican Republic, Rafael Trujillo, ordered 20,000 blacks killed because they could not pronounce the letter "r" in 'perejil', the Spanish word for parsley. Throughout history, such horrors have been witnessed. Write about an historical tragedy or a recent one.

~ Day 6~

An Ode to Parsley ~ Author Unknown

"Parsley, oh parsley, you wondrous herb!
You raise any dish's caliber from just mediocre to superb!
With bright green leaves, curly or flat,

Your versatility amazes us, and we are grateful for
that.
You freshen our breath just when we need it most,
Like if we eat too much garlic, or a big, heavy roast.
And you keep us healthy and strong, with vitamins
A, B, and C,
Plus calcium and iron, too – all that, completely fat-
free!
Those ancient Greeks knew of your worth, crowning
winners with your leaves,
Figuring you good enough for mere mortals if you
were good enough for Hercules.
And those Romans found use for you even when
facing death,
Sprinkling you to freshen corpses, just like you
freshen our breath!
Yes, your wonders are many, and without you no
chef could live.
If it seems we take you granted sometimes, we ask
you to forgive.
For we know that without you, there'd be no bouquet
garni,
And the world would have to live without wonderful
tabbouleh.
You're the ultimate team player, helping other foods
excel and bask in glory.
But while they may get all the fame, do not doubt that
we know the true story.
For without you, they'd be just another soup, another
vegetable on the plate.
But it is thanks to your panache that they meet
another fate...
They rise to culinary heights previously unknown,

Then take all the credit with an ego quite overblown.
So, dear parsley, with eternal gratitude we offer you our praise,
And with reverence most high, to you our toast we raise!"

Choose a line and use it as your writing prompt for today. Or write your own Ode to Parsley!

~Day 7~

The well-known song "*Scarborough Fair*" by Simon and Garfunkle begins:

"Are you going to Scarborough Fair?
Parsley, Sage, Rosemary and Thyme
Remember me to one who lives there
She once was a true love of mine"

Write your own song about going to a fair.

Plantain

The botanical name for plantain is Plantago major.
The leaves are antibacterial, astringent, anti-
inflammatory, an expectorant and can help stop
bleeding. Plantain has been used for asthma, coughs,
ulcers, irritable bowel, fevers and to get rid of worms
and intestinal parasites. I use it for bug bites or any
skin irritation.

~Day 1~

"Plantain works to sooth your soul just like it works to sooth the skin." ~ Garliq. Write about soothing your soul.

~Day 2~

Often plantain is found on or along well used dirt trails. It seems to like being walked on and growing in very hard packed soil. Write about walking on an old dirt trail. How did this trail come to be?

~Day 3~

Native Americans called plantain 'white man's footsteps' because it followed them as they spread over the continent. Europeans brought it with them when they immigrated to North America. Write about something that you have taken with you whenever you move to a new place. Or, if you have not ever moved, what would you take with you? Or write about following someone in their footsteps!

~Day 4~

Plantain is also known as: buckhorn, cart track plant, cuckoo's bread, dooryard plant, healing blade, hen plant, lambs foot, mother-die, ripple grass, roadweed, snakeweed, soldier's herb, and waybread. Write a poem using as many of these names as you can.

~Day 5~

Long ago, plantain was believed to be a protective plant being carried to protect against the dangers of travel such as snake-bites. In Ireland it is associated with St. Patrick who is also associated with getting rid of snakes. Write a short story about snakes or the dangers of travel or St. Patrick or Ireland! Or see if you can write a short story about snakes and the dangers of travel and St. Patrick and Ireland!

~Day 6~

You can find tons of folk-lore telling about plantain as a first aid herb to use 'on the spot'. Plantain is sometimes called the "band aid" plant. It is helpful for bug bites, poison ivy, sunburn, eczema and diaper rash. One of the handiest ways to treat these skin irritations is with a "spit poultice" made from plantain. Basically, you a leaf, chew it up a bit, spit it out and place on your injured area until it starts to feel better. You can also use a plantain spit poultice to pull a splinter to the surface of the skin, making it easier to extract. Write about your skin.

~Day 7~

The Story of Plantain from *A Kids Herb Book* by Leslie Tierra:

"Once there was a fluffy cloud that lived high in the sky. Every so often the cloud would grow dark as it filled with water from the earth and then uncontrollably rain upon all the plants and creatures below. Now the cloud could have lived happily ever after just like all the other clouds in the sky, except one day it realized it could not be fully happy so long as someone below was unhappy. This usually happened when Cloud released rain when people were not ready for it. Cloud was silly to wish that it could only rain when everyone was ready because it is impossible for everyone to be happy at the same time. So, no matter what, Cloud was left no choice but to feel unhappy every time it released a shower. One day Cloud thought long and hard about this problem. It heard a rumor going around in the heavens. The news spread from stars to the moon, and the moon to the planets that a special event was about to happen. This rumor was that the sun and moon were going to shine together at the same time. Now this event meant that there was opportunity for magic to occur. When Cloud realized this, it suddenly had a brilliant idea. Cloud would use this magic to give a special gift to the people in exchange for the good times they missed when it rained. When the day arrived, Cloud took special position in the sky so that it could cover a large area. Then, at the exact moment sun and moon carefully beamed all their rays into the cloud, filling it with light instead of water. When Cloud was so stuffed it could hold no longer, the magic happened. Cloud burst open and showered down special seeds instead of water. Where ever this special cloud seed landed it sprouted up. It had ribs like the rays of the sun and moon. A long stem held a crown of tiny white flowers that seemed to reflect light back to the skies. This was a magical plant, for it had many healing properties. Now these plants began to spread everywhere and people began to treat them like weeds. They did not eat it because it did not taste good enough, and they wouldn't pick the flowers because they were too small and not as attractive as the rose or peony bush. People began to curse this plant and poison or yank it from the ground. They would yell at this plant "why do you grow where I am planting, planting, planting?" (See how fast you can say planting, planting, planting. See how it changes to plantain). When Cloud saw how this plant did not change the people's happiness, he realized some people choose to be happy and receptive and others become closed and unhappy even with a special gift. But then Cloud saw that some people did appreciate the gift as they used it for injuries, stings, slivers and a blood purifier. It was magic after all. The End."

Write about magic!

Red Clover

The botanical name for red clover is Trifolium pretense. Russian folk healers and traditional Chinese medicine have used red clover for decades for asthma and bronchitis. In recent times red clover extracts have been used to help hormonal imbalances such as during menopause. It is commonly used to treat eczema and psoriasis.

~Day 1~

"A best friend is like a four leaf clover: hard to find and lucky to have." ~ Unknown. Write a letter to your best friend and mail it!

~Day 2~

A tradition is that clover is the favorite plant of the fairies. Holding clover in your hand is thought to help you to see fairies. Write a short fairy tale which includes red clovers.

~Day 3~

"I'll love you till the bluebells forget to bloom; I'll love you till the clover has lost its perfume. I'll love you till the poets run out of rhyme, Until the twelfth of never and that's a long, long time." ~ Paul Webster. Use this as a springboard for your writing, "I'll love you till..........."

~Day 4~

Dreaming of clover is considered, of course, good luck. Walking through healthy clover fields in dreams means that all the things the dreamer desires will come to pass. Make a list of 31 things you desire. If today is the 29th day of the month and you listed "*a visit with my sister*" as the 29th thing on your list, write about *a visit with your sister*.

~Day 5~

"Never iron a four-leaf clover. You wouldn't want to press your luck." ~ Unknown. Write your own joke(s) about clover or ironing?

~Day 6~

"Heart of my heart, we cannot die!

Love triumphant in flower and tree,

Every life that laughs at the sky

Tells us nothing can cease to be:

One, we are one with the song today,

One with the clover that scents the world,

One with the Unknown, far away,

One with the stars, when earth grows old."

~ Alfred Noyes

What comes to mind for you when you read this poem? Is there a line that grabs you?

~Day 7~

Edward Martin Sr. from Cooper Landing, Alaska, USA, currently has the largest four-leaf clover collection according to the Guiness Book of Records. Previously, George Kaminski, a Pennsylvania prisoner had managed to find 72,927 four-leaf clovers from prison yards. Kaminski died while still incarcerated in February 2008 after a transfer to a clover-free prison. Do you have a collection of anything? Write about your collection, or if you don't, write about why you do not collect things!

Rose

One botanical name for wild rose is Rosa acicularis. I say *one* botanical name because there are really many, many botanical names for the various different types of roses! Rose oil can improve acne and depression. It is thought to relieve anxiety and rosacea. Some consider it to naturally increase libido. According to the Arthritis Foundation, rose hips seem to reduce arthritis-associated inflammation.

~Day 1~

The Persian word *gul* for rose has some special interest for folks from the state of Kentucky. During the Kentucky Derby horse race, also known as the "Run for the Roses," it is an old tradition to drink mint juleps. The Old French word julep comes from the Middle Latin *julapium* which comes from the Arabic *julab* which comes from Persian *gulab* meaning "rose water." Have you ever been to a horse race? Capture the moment with words. Or, if not, maybe use the line "run for the roses" to inspire your writing today!

~Day 2~

The rose is known as the flower of love. Write a letter to someone you love (be certain to include a reference to roses) and mail it!

~Day 3~

"A rose is a rose is a rose" ~ Gertrude Stein. Use this line as a springboard for your writing, "A rose is ...."

~Day 4~

Fossil records show that roses have been around prior to the existence of humans. One of the oldest rose fossil dates back approximately 30-35 million years. Create an alpha poem using the word "fossil".

~Day 5~

According to legend, Flora, the Roman goddess of flowers, came upon the lifeless body of a beautiful nymph in the woods. She decided to give the nymph a new life as a flower that would be more beautiful than any other. Flora placed a crown of dewdrops upon her new creation and named her 'Rose, queen of flowers.' Imagine that Rose awakens. Write about what happens when Rose and Flora meet.

~Day 6~

"Roses are red, Violets are blue, Sugar is sweet, and so are you." ~ Traditional nursery rhyme. Create a new version! "Roses are red, violets are blue, _____ and _____!"

~Day 7~

"We can complain because rose bushes have thorns, or rejoice because thorn bushes have roses." ~ Abraham Lincoln .

It's sort of like viewing the glass as half empty or half full, right? Write about being a pessimist or about being an optimist.

Rosemary

The botanical name for rosemary is Rosmarinus officinalis. Rosemary is known to prevent hair loss and encourage the growth of healthy hair. Traditionally, rosemary has been used for its ability to help with gastrointestinal complaints. Rosemary aromatherapy can reduce the level of cortisol (the hormone produced by stress). A cup of Rosemary tea can relieve headaches as well as an aspirin.

~Day 1~

"There's rosemary, that's for remembrance. Pray you, love, remember." ~ William Shakespeare. Write about someone, some thing, some place or some experience that you never want to forget.

~Day 2~

"In our everyday garden grow the rosemary, juniper, ferns and plane trees, perfectly tangible and visible. For these plants that have an illusory relationship with us, which in no way alters their existentiality, we are merely an event, an accident, and our presence, which seems so solid, laden with gravity, is to them no more than a momentary void in motion through the air. Reality is a quality that belongs to them, and we can exercise no rights over it." ~ Leo Lionni. Follow your thoughts about this reading with your words.

~Day 3~

"She wished she had a little yellow house of her own, with a flower box full of real flowers and herbs – pansies and rosemary – and a sweet lover who would swing dance with her in the evenings and cook pasta and read poetry aloud." ~ Francesca Lia Block. Make a list of 31 wishes. Then, if today is the first day of the month and you listed *Good Health* as your number one wish, write about *Good Health*.

~Day 4~

"Where rosemary flourishes the lady rules." ~ Old folklore. Write about what it would be like if the world were ruled by women.

~Day 5~

In one version of the fairy tale, *Sleeping Beauty*, it was said that she was awoken from her sleep when Prince Charming brushed a rosemary sprig over her cheek. Write your own version of the Sleeping Beauty fairy tale. Or make up an entirely new fairy tale!

~Day 6~

"There are some things I know for certain: always throw spilled salt over your left shoulder; keep rosemary by your garden gate; plant lavender for luck; and fall in love whenever you can." ~ Alice Hoffman. Write about some things that you know for certain.

~Day 7~

Currently, one of the most well-known herbalists is Rosemary Gladstar. She is known as "The Godmother of American Herbalism." She's written 12 best-selling herbal books, taught thousands of folks about herbs, started two herb stores and a school. Write a letter to Rosemary Gladstar thanking her for her contributions to herbalism and mail it! Send it to her in care of Sage Mountain Herbal Education Center: PO Box 420, East Barre VT, 05649.

Sage

The botanical name for common sage is Salvia officinalis. The Latin name for sage, *salvia*, means 'to heal'. It has been used as an antibiotic and an antifungal. Some other possible healing benefits of sage include reducing dandruff, helping to regulate menstruation, reducing night sweats and headaches, to ease joint pain and indigestion, as a gargle for sore throats and finally, against colds and coughs.

~Day 1~

"In the grand opera of cooking, sage represents an easily offended and capricious prima donna. It likes to have the stage almost to itself." ~ Anonymous. Write about a prima donna, someone who wants all of the attention.

~Day 2~

"He that would live for aye, must eat sage in May" ~ an English proverb. Eating a sage leaf on the first day of May is believed to promote a long and healthy life. There are many other traditions associated with May Day, such as May baskets and May poles. Have you ever celebrated May Day? If so, write about what you do on the first of May. Or, if not, invent your own idea of what you might do on the next May Day.

~Day 3~

The Legend of the Sage Plant is an ancient story about the mother of Jesus when she was fleeing to save the life of her baby. It goes something like this......Utterly helpless and scared for her child's life, Mary asked a nearby rose plant for a place to hide but the plant refused any kind of refuge for fear of being crushed by the angry soldiers; it is believed that the rose plant started bearing thorns since then. Mother Mary then turned to the clove bush for refuge but to no avail as the plant was too busy blooming; it is said that since then, the clove plant has been blooming flowers that give out a bad scent. The only bush that remained now was the sage plant and it was very kind and offered to help mother Mary. It quickly blossomed and created a shelter for the mother and the child. When the soldiers passed them by without any suspicion, Mary, in her gratitude, thanked and blessed the plant saying, 'Sage, oh holy sage, many thanks. I bless you for your good deed which everyone will henceforth remember'. Since then, the sage plant has been revered for its healing powers and it is a common ingredient in Christmas stuffing. Write your own story/poem/song about kindness or about giving shelter.

~Day 4~

"Why should a man die when sage grows in the garden?" ~ Latin proverb. Use this as a springboard for your writing, "When sage grows in the garden, _____".

~Day 5~

An excerpt from a poem by Fady Joudah titled "*The Tea and Sage Poem*":

"Because the earth knows
   The scent of history,
   It gave the people sage."

Use the first line to begin your writing. "Because the earth knows, _____".

~Day 6~

Here are some lines from another poem titled "*Sage*" by Rachel Astarte:

"Once, I worked making dinner salads
in a family restaurant outside of Philadelphia
with a crazy artist who swigged Chablis
as she cooked the evening specials.
At the busiest time of the night, she burned sage —
held it to the grill and smudged it against the metal stove.
She did this, she said, "to soothe us."

So, for a few minutes, among quick-fried garlic
and hungry accountants there in the air
was the heavy earth-smell of history, of wisdom."

Choose any words or any line from this poem to
inspire your writing.

~Day 7~

The herbalist Maud Grieve, writing during the Great
Depression, described how "country people" in her
time used to eat fresh sage leaves with bread and
butter: "there is no better and more wholesome way
of taking it." The idiom "your bread and butter"
refers to supplying the basic needs of life. What is
your bread and butter?

Tarragon

The botanical name for tarragon is Artemisia dracunculus.
Tarragon has strong effects on the nervous and digestive
system, and can help overcome things like toothaches,
digestive issues, bacterial infections, menstruation issues
and insomnia. In large amounts, tarragon can possibly
slow blood clotting. If you are going to undergo surgery,
stop taking tarragon at least two weeks before a scheduled
surgery to prevent any bleeding issues.

~Day 1~

"I believe that if ever I had to practice cannibalism, I might manage if there were enough tarragon around." ~ James Beard. This well-know chef clearly loves using tarragon for flavoring! Beard was passionate about American cuisine. He mentored generations of professional chefs and gourmands. He had a television show called "I Love to Eat"! Make a list of 31 things that you love to eat. If today is the 2nd day of the month and you listed *potatoes* as the 2nd thing on your list, write about your love of *potatoes*!

~Day 2~

"To write a tarragon ode, you might address the effects this fine herb has on the expansive senses." ~ the first line from a poem by Caroline Knox titled *"Tarragon"*. Write an ode to tarragon.

~Day 3~

"It's spring and spring is glorious; brings the child right out of me.

Makes me want to dance at midnight beneath budding apple trees." ~ the last line from a poem by Faye Lanham Gibson titled *"The Tansy and the Tarragon"*. Write about spring!

~Day 4~

"Nothing speaks more accurately to the complexity of life than food. Who has not had, let us say, a béarnaise, the child of hollandaise, and has not come away from the taste of it feeling overwhelmed? At first, it fills the mouth with the softness of butter and then the richness of egg, and before it becomes too rich or too comfortable, the moment shifts and begins to ground itself in darkness with the root of a shallot and the hint of crushed peppercorn. But then, the taste deepens. The memory of rebirth is made manifest with the sacred chervil, sweet and grassy with a note of licorice, whose spring scent is so like myrrh that it recalls the gift of the Wise Men and the holy birth whenever it is tasted. And then, of course, the "King of Herbs," tarragon with its gentle licorice, reminds us not to forget that miracles are possible.

And just when we think we understand what we are experiencing, the taste turns again on the tongue, and finishes with shrill vinegar followed by a reduction of wine so that the acid tempers the sauce but never dominates." ~ N.M. Kelby.

What luscious language! You could close your eyes, point at the page and see where your finger lands. I did it just now and landed on *"with a note of licorice"*. Write about what ever you find when you blindly point at this lovely essay.

~Day 5~

"The first thing I made for you, so many years ago: tarragon chicken sammy on fresh baked bread. My apartment. A very personal, very special memory. (Excusing the dangling participle in this instance because the intent of the words far outweighs my need to be grammatically correct). ~ Heather Poston. Write about being grammatically incorrect. Or, if you prefer, write a persuasive note about the importance of correct grammar.

~Day 6~

Tarragon's name is taken from the French *esdragon*, which means 'little dragon' because of its serpent-like root system, which will completely strangle the plant if it is not divided often enough. Write a short story (or a song, or a poem or a play) about little dragons.

~Day 7~

According to those who interpret dreams, tarragon represents toxic people around you. Dreaming of tarragon means that there is someone close to you who is not what they seem. Tarragon symbolizes betrayal. If you dream of tarragon, it is a warning to be careful of who you trust. Have you ever been betrayed? Or found out that someone was not who you thought they were? Write a limerick about betrayal or falsity. A limerick is a humorous poem consisting of five lines. The first, second, and fifth lines must have seven to ten syllables while rhyming and having the same verbal rhythm. The third and fourth lines only have to have five to seven syllables, and have to rhyme with each other and have the same rhythm. Here is an example:

A Young Lady of Lynn   by Anonymous

"There was a young lady of Lynn,
Who was so uncommonly thin
That when she essayed
To drink lemonade
She slipped through the straw and fell in."

Thyme

The botanical name for thyme is Thymus Vulgaris. Thyme oil is antiseptic, antibacterial, and has calming properties. It helps women with menstrual and menopausal symptoms. Thyme has been found beneficial for reducing the likelihood of stroke, relieving arthritis symptoms, fighting fungal and bacterial infections, and soothing skin conditions.

~Day 1~

"Just as bees make honey from thyme, the strongest and driest of herbs, so do the wise profit from the most difficult of experiences. " ~ Plato . Write about when you went through a difficult time and it ended up being good for you.

~Day 2~

"Strange things can be thought by little girls who lie in the cloudy softness of wild thyme, and sometimes those thoughts can lead to dreams that take us far away into places we have never been." ~ Sharon Brown. Write about thoughts that lead to dreams.

~Day 3~

"Nature has not changed. The night is still unsullied, the stars still twinkle, and the wild thyme smells as sweetly now as it did then ... We may be afflicted and unhappy, but no one can take from us the sweet delight which is nature's gift to those who love her and her poetry." ~ George Sand. Write a thank you letter to Nature for the gifts she has given you.

~Day 4~

"My favorite comfort food would have to be braised beef. You know, beef, slow-cooked in a Dutch oven or in a slow cooker until it falls apart with simple mushrooms, some onions and lots of fresh thyme and garlic." ~ Tyler Florence. What is your most favorite comfort food? Write another thank you letter, this time, to your favorite comfort food!

~Day 5~

"They lay on their heathery beds and listened to all the sounds of the night. They heard the little grunt of a hedgehog going by. They saw the flicker of bats overhead. They smelt the drifting scent of honeysuckle, and the delicious smell of wild thyme crushed under their bodies. A reed-warbler sang a beautiful little song in the reeds below, and then another answered." ~ Enid Blyton . Go outside at night and listen to the sounds. Smell the smells. Then, write about it.

~Day 6~

"But what will you keep

When you can't even rhyme?

Sleep, my dear, sleep

And a handful of thyme."

~ The last verse in a poem titled *A Handful of Thyme* by May Sarton. Write a poem about sleep that does not rhyme.

~Day 7~

The origins of the word thyme are from Greek word *thymon* meaning courage. Write a haiku about courage. Here is a haiku I wrote.....

"Sunny afternoon
A flat, courageous rock stands
whilst watching a bowl"

Tumeric

The botanical name for turmeric is Curcuma longa.
Throughout Asia, turmeric tea is known by some as
"liquid gold." Turmeric works to improve your
health, by reducing inflammation, aiding digestion,
improving the health of your heart and strengthening
your bones. Turmeric has so many actions on so
many systems that you could say the whole body can
feel its effects.

~Day 1~

"The moon is yellow as mustard stain by turmeric." ~ Fritz Purdum. Use this as a springboard for your writing, "The moon is _____".

~Day 2~

"Each spice has a special day to it. For turmeric it is Sunday, when light drips fat and butter-colored into the bins to be soaked up glowing, when you pray to the nine planets for love and luck." ~ Chitra Banerjee Divakaruni . What is *your* special day of the week? Write about your special day.

~Day 3~

An excerpt from yet another poem, this one titled *Freak Storm* by Freddie Johnson:

"Turmeric field drowned…….

No curry tonight."

Write about a story about a storm that interfered with dinner plans! Or write about curry!

~Day 4~

Here are a few lines from a poem titled *Feeling Rough* by Jenny Linsel:

"Sore throat, runny nose,
Could be a cold I suppose,
Or could it be influenza?
I think I need a detox cleanser
Turmeric, folic acid, gingko leaf
I'm feeling rough beyond belief"

Write your own poem about feeling rough.

~Day 5~

"Khandoba (a Hindu God) is typically depicted with four arms, one of which holds a 'Bhandara-patra' or a bowl of turmeric powder — the essence of the Bhandara festival that is held in Jejuri, 50km from Pune, Maharashtra. Every Somavati Amavasya (new moon that falls on a Monday), devotees of Khandoba gather at the magnificent Jejuri temple with tonnes of turmeric, smearing it on each other and throwing it all around amid energetic singing and dancing. The temple-town earned the 'Sonyachi Jejuri' (golden Jejuri) tag, thanks to this colourful celebration." ~ Prachi Moghe. Create your own celebration using turmeric. Capture it with words!

~Day 6~

"The journey
from my home to my palace
from the hive to the flower
from my veins to my heart
felt like
I was returning to my dreams
returning to the unknown
returning home

salt turned to turmeric
jeans turned to silk
water turned to lassi
cars transformed into rickshaws
the rain falling from the bleak sky
turned to crimson powers
falling out of the sky on Holi"

An excerpt from *Salt to Turmeric − A Poem on the Spirit of India* by Shreya Sharma. Choose any line or image or word from this poem to inspire your own words.

~Day 7~

Most of the production of Turmeric (approximately 90%) is in India. An old folktale from India goes that there was once a very pretty girl called Kusumba Kohli. Narayan, (known more widely as Vishnu), fell in love with her and came to meet her secretly. But Kusumba's was already married. Her husband, Kaindhu Kohli, found out and chased after Narayan. Kaindhu was a strong and determined young man. Narayan had to run very fast. He tried to hide in a patch of colocasia (arbi) that grew above ground in those days. But its broad leaves shook in fright and Narayan's hiding place was discovered. You failed me; may you grow underground hereafter," said Narayan to the arbi, and ran on to hide behind a banana tree. But the slender banana tree could not hide Narayan. "May you bear fruit but once a year, on just one stem," scolded Narayan, and ran to hide behind some rocks. A dog napping there was startled and began barking and Narayan had to run again. "You're not a bad creature but stones will come your way for talking too much," said Narayan angrily and he ran on. Kaindhu was gaining ground and Narayan was growing desperate. He ran down a hill and threw himself into a leafy patch of wild turmeric. The long leaves closed gently over him and stayed still as Kaindhu went pounding by. When it was safe to emerge, Narayan blessed the turmeric. "You shall have a place of honour at every wedding and auspicious event. No happy ceremony can take place without you," he said.

Write your own folktale about turmeric.

Valerian

The botanical name for valerian is Valeriana officinalis. Valerian contains many healing properties, in particular for insomnia due to its relaxation and sedative effects. It's often found in combination with chamomile in a tea. This calming effect has made valerian a natural remedy for anxiety as well.

~Day 1~

Valerian is calming to humans, but excites mice. In the legend of the *Pied Piper of Hamlin*, he baited the rodents with valerian to drive them out of the city. Write your own legend about valerian.

~Day 2~

The name Valerian is from the Latin word *valere* which means 'to be healthy'. Hippocrates claimed "The wise man should consider that health is the greatest of human blessings. Let food be your medicine." Write about food as medicine.

~Day 3~

For those interested in making magic, valerian is used in spells for: protection, purification, harmony, peace, happiness, love, creative work, and to attract abundance. To my way of thinking, magic is simply the act of setting an intention. You can burn candles or drink some valerian tea. Then, set your intention. For example, "I intend to do what I love with the people I love in the places I love. So be it!". Write your own magic spell or intention!

~Day 4~

Cats are attracted to catnip. Cats are also fond of valerian root. Do a 5-minute writing spring about cats!

~Day 5~

"Picking up my sandals,

I walk up the beach

under the bridge

past crimson valerian

It's balmy perfume

scenting a delicious day"

~ the last verse in a poem titled *A Delicious Day* by Eiken Laan. Write your own poem or short story about a delicious day.

~Day 6~

During World War II, valerian was used in England to alleviate the stress brought on by air raids. What do you do to alleviate stress in your life? Maybe journaling? If you have been following this book from the beginning until now, you have done lots of creative, expressive writing. Is this a stress relief for you, or not? Write about writing.

~Day 7~

The language of flowers is known as floriography. During the Victorian era, people would exchange small nosegays. Each flower symbolized a certain sentiment. Valerian represents an accommodating disposition. Who do you know who has an accommodating disposition? Write a character sketch about this person.

Sweet Violet

The botanical name for sweet violets is Viola odorata. Syrup made from violets is employed as a laxative. Violet leaves are an old popular remedy for bruises. They also contain salicylic acid that is a natural sort of aspirin.

~Day 1~

"Yesterday I sat in a field of violets for a long time perfectly still, until I really sank into it - into the rhythm of the place, I mean - then when I got up to go home I couldn't walk quickly or evenly because I was still in time with the field." ~ Anne Morrow Lindbergh. Find someplace to sit for a while and then write about the rhythm of that place.

~Day 2~

Violet is the diminutive form of the Latin *Viola*, the Latin form of the Greek name Ione. There is a legend that when Jupiter changed his beloved Ione into a white heifer for fear of Juno's jealousy, he caused these modest flowers to spring forth from the earth to be fitting food for her, and he gave them her name. Imagine that you meet Jealousy at a local coffee shop. What sort of a character is Jealousy (other than being generally jealous!). Write about your conversation.

~Day 3~

The violet plays a central role in a different love story, this one from England:

"King Frost felt lonely in his huge ice palace where everything was frozen and lifeless. He thereupon sent his agents out to look for a lovely girl to melt his heart and bring him happiness. There were many beautiful women, but they, too, were cold and icy in their appearance and demeanor. The search continued until a shy maiden named Violet was found and presented to the king. He immediately came under the spell of her charm and sweetness and fell deeply in love with her. Although once a strict and passionless ruler, he slowly became gentle and warmhearted and vowed to his people that the harsh and endless winters of his realm would become milder for one half of each year. Such was the tender effect that Violet had upon him. But Violet missed her family and friends. She pleaded with the king to allow her to see her people again. Because of his love for her, he granted her wish to visit them each spring. His only condition was that she could only return to them in the form of a flower for part of the year, coming back to her husband's icy realm each winter."

Write about the spell of charm and sweetness. They say that you can attract more flies with honey than with vinegar. If you were going to teach someone to be charming and sweet, what would your lesson look like?

~Day 4~

"We may pass violets looking for roses. We may pass contentment looking for victory." ~ Bernard Williams. Write about contentment.

~Day 5~

In 1791, the last year of his life, Mozart wrote a piece called *Sehnsucht nach dem Fruhlinge ("Longing for Spring")*, based on a poem about violets written by Christian Christoph Sturm (1740-1786). Even today, "Longing for Spring" is still a favorite among German-speaking children:

"Come, dear May and turn the trees to verdant green
  and make the little violets blossom by the brook!
How gladly I would see a violet one again, dear May
  how I would like once more to take a walk!
But most of all I feel for Charlotte in her grief;
  the poor girl just sits there and longs for blossom time.
In vain I fetch some toys to help her pass the time
  she sits upon her stool just like a broody hen...
If only it got warmer and the grass began to grow!
Do come, dear May, we children do beg you earnestly!
Do come and, above all, bring lots of violets
  and also nightingales and pretty cuckoo birds!. "

If you were sad and brooding, would you like a little bouquet of violets? Write a letter to yourself to lift your spirits. Then, next time you are sad, read it.

~Day 6~

"Within my heart a garden grows, wild with violets and fragrant rose. bright daffodils line the narrow path, my footsteps silent as i pass. sweet tulips nod their heads in rest; i kneel in prayer to seek gods best. for round my garden a fence stands firm to guard my heart so i can learn who should enter, and who should wait on the other side of my locked gate. i clasp the key around my neck and wonder if the time is yet. if i unlocked the gate today, would you come in? or run away?" ~ Robin Jones Gunn. What phrase or words grab you? Grab your pencil and go!

~Day 7~

A poem, *The Violet,* by Jane Taylor (1783-1824), is included in a book titled *Poems That Every Child Should Know* edited by Mary E. Burt.

"DOWN in a green and shady bed
□A modest violet grew;
Its stalk was bent, it hung its head,
□As if to hide from view.

And yet it was a lovely flower,
□No colours bright and fair;
It might have graced a rosy bower,
□Instead of hiding there.

Yet there it was content to bloom;
□In modest tints arrayed;
And there diffused its sweet perfume,
□Within the silent shade.

Then let me to the valley go,
□This pretty flower to see;
That I may also learn to grow
□In sweet humility."

Write about humility.

Wormwood

The botanical name for common wormwood is Artemisia absinthium . Wormwood has been used to treat jaundice, parasites and gout. Common wormwood has been used for digestive system, liver and bladder ailments. Wormwood for pain-relief when applied externally as a tincture rubbed on the skin or a compress placed over the painful area.

~Day 1~

Wormwood is sometimes called "old woman". Capture with words the last time you spent with an old woman.

~Day 2~

Long ago, it was believed that wormwood was the antidote for the bite of a sea dragon. Imagine that you go to the beach, carrying a spring of wormwood to be on the safe side, and meet a sea dragon. Write up your conversation with this creature. What do you and the sea dragon talk about?

~Day 3~

In the past (and maybe still today?), Mexicans celebrated their festival of the Goddess of Salt by a ceremonial dance with women wearing garlands made of wormwood on their heads. Salt has been treasured since ancient times. Humans must have some form of salt to survive. Salt was one of the main ways to preserve food before the invention of refrigeration. Write an ode to salt! Or create your own special holiday to celebrate salt! Would your celebration include wormwood in some way?

~Day 4~

Wormwood is one of the major ingredients in absinthe, an intoxicating drink associated with the death of the writer Edgar Allan Poe and the suicide of the painter Vincent Van Gogh. Poe noted, "I was never *really* insane, except on occasions where my heart was touched." And Van Gogh also spoke about the heart, The heart of man is very much like the sea, it has its storms, it has its tides and in its depths it has its pearls too." Write about the heart.

~Day 5~

Wormwood prevents insects from damaging clothing. Write about your favorite article of clothing. Describe it in detail. Tell about the places this piece of clothing has been with you.

~Day 6~

"Some nights are like honey - and some like wine - and some like wormwood." ~ Lucy Maud Montgomery. Use this line as a springboard for your writing. "Some nights are like………".

~Day 7~

"On rolls the stream with a perpetual sigh;
The rocks moan wildly as it passes by;
Hyssop and wormwood border all the strand,
And not a flower adorns the dreary land." ~ William C. Bryant .

Suddenly, you can hear and understand what the stream is sighing and what the rocks are moaning. Write about what you learn.

Yarrow

The botanical name for yarrow is Achillea
millefolium. Yarrow tea is a good remedy for severe
colds. Yarrow is considered a general tonic for the
cardio-vascular system. Yarrow has been used for
internal wounds in the digestive tract.

~Day 1~

Yarrow was found amongst other herbs in a Neanderthal burial site which dates from around 60,000 BC. Would you like to have herbs buried or cremated with you? Write about what herbs you would want and why!

~Day 2~

The Chinese use bundles of 64 long, straight yarrow sticks to read the hexagrams associated with the *I Ching*, a system of divination or predicting the future. Would you like to know what the future holds for you? If you could have it your way, write about your hopes for your future.

~Day 3~

Yarrow is also known as allheal, bad man's plaything, bloodwort, carpenter's weed, dog daisy, nosebleed, old man's mustard, old man's pepper, soldier's woundwort, squirrel's tail, stanchweed, thousand-leaf, and woundwort. Use one or more of these other names for yarrow in your writing today.

~Day 4~

Here is the first verse in a poem titled *A Song for Yarrow* by Walter Elliot:

"A song for Yarrow. How to start?
It must be written from the heart,
And how to tell in one short tale
The story of the Yarrow vale?"

Write a song or a short tale about yarrow, from your heart.

~Day 5~

"Helps to clarify boundaries between people: particularly useful for those who are easily influenced and depleted by others and their environment. It is for those who easily absorb negative influences, and may be prone to allergies and environmental illness. By 'astringing' the boundaries around a person and preventing their energies from 'bleeding' into their environment, it acts to strengthen and solidify the self, the essence, allowing and enhancing their ability to heal, teach, counsel or follow their chosen path." ~ Anne McIntyre shares about yarrow. Write about how you take care to protect yourself from negative energies.

~Day 6~

"In creative projects, yarrow reminds us to move with careful and steady intention. Yarrow magic is the magic of regulating the creative flow, the blood of our work. In this, Yarrow is complex, guiding us toward managing our energies as they come in and as they flow out with careful precision. Yarrow teaches us to draw energy from our environment as she draws her energy from the hot, dry, sunny climates she likes best, to store that energy and later to use it to regulate and shape our passion as we create." ~ Candace Hunter. Be creative and write about creativity!

~Day 7~

Legend has it that when the Greek hero Achilles was born, his mother held him by the heel and dipped him into a tub of yarrow tea to protect him from harm. He eventually died due to a battle wound on the ankle, where according to the story the yarrow did not touch. Whether there is any truth to this tale about his birth, yarrow was Achilles's most trusted herbal medicine. He used it to staunch and disinfect his soldier's wounds, popularizing its use in his time and leading to its genus name Achillea. Record what you know about your own birth or the birth of someone who is dear to you.

About the Author

Iris is..........

~ a mother and a grandmother

~a gardener and herbalist

~a nationally certified poetry and journaling therapist

~a good friend

~a traveler

~in love

You can reach her via email at irisgarden9@gmail.com

Made in the USA
Middletown, DE
06 May 2019